The Optimism Gap

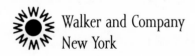

Walker and Company
New York

The Optimism Gap

The I'm OK–
They're Not Syndrome
and the Myth of
American Decline

David Whitman

Foreword by Christopher Jencks

For Lynn and Lily

First published in the United States of America in 1998
by Walker Publishing Company, Inc.

Published simultaneously in Canada by
Thomas Allen & Son Canada, Limited, Markham, Ontario

Library of Congress Cataloging-in-Publication Data
Whitman, David.
The optimism gap: the I'm ok–they're not syndrome and the myth
of American decline / David Whitman; foreword by
Christopher Jencks.
p. cm.
Includes bibliographical references.
ISBN 0-8027-1334-3 (alk. paper)
1. Public opinion—United States.   2. United States—Social
conditions—1980—Public opinion.   3. Quality of life—United
States—Public opinion.   4. Social problems—United States—Public
opinion.   5. Optimism—United States.   6. Pessimism—United States.
I. Title.
HN90.P8W45   1998   98-15694
303.3'8'0973—dc21   CIP

Book design by Ralph L. Fowler

Printed in the United States of America

2   4   6   8   10   9   7   5   3   1

CONTENTS

Like every American, I learned in high school that democracy required an informed electorate, capable of making sensible choices between candidates and policies. Not until a decade later, when I embarked on a short-lived career as a journalist, did I discover how few of my fellow citizens had taken this injunction to heart. Reading public opinion surveys, I found that while Americans had opinions on almost every political issue, they seldom knew even the most basic facts about the choices confronting their elected representatives. Worst yet, much of what people thought they knew was wrong. This situation has not changed. In 1995, when the economy had been growing steadily for more than three years, most Americans thought the country was still in a recession. They also thought that crime, which had been falling for several years, was rising. Errors of this kind are not inconsequential. Worries about the economy and fear of crime are important determinants of how Americans vote.

Much of the misinformation that infects the American political system follows systematic patterns. *The Optimism Gap* examines one such pattern: Americans' assumption that things were better in the past than they are today and that the country is now headed in the wrong direction. David Whitman, one of America's best-informed journalists, has assembled an extraordinary range of evidence about the pervasiveness of such beliefs. He finds two seemingly contradictory views. On the one hand, most Americans say that they and their family are doing extremely well. By this standard, we are among the most optimistic people on earth. On the other hand, most Americans think the rest of the country is in deep trouble on almost every front. Crime, drug abuse, moral standards, public education, job security, poverty, hunger, homelessness, and health care are all getting worse.

Whitman then asks a question that pollsters and political scientists seldom ask: Are the public's beliefs correct? In some cases the answer is ambiguous. Crime rates, for example, are higher today than in the 1950s but lower than in the 1970s. In principle, that should make baby boomers who grew up in the 1950s think crime has risen, while their children should think it has fallen. In reality, however, everyone thinks crime has risen. In other cases our sense of national decline is pure fantasy. There is no evidence, for example, that public schools teach children less today than in the past. National testing programs show that the schools teach most students more than they used to.

We all tend to romanticize the past. When we were children, our parents protected us from uncomfortable facts and risks, and moral choices seemed simple. Looking back on this simpler time, we then imagine that the world we experienced was the world our parents experienced. Compared to our present adult world, the old days look pretty good. Until relatively recently, however, this kind of nostalgia was partially offset by widespread optimism about the future. Almost everything American was supposed to be bigger and better, and whatever wasn't soon would be. Most Americans worried more about troublemakers who wanted to subvert the "American way of life" than about fundamental flaws in American institutions or American character. No longer. Both liberal and conservative politicians and activists now assume that playing Cassandra will draw a bigger audience than playing Pollyanna. Partly for that reason and partly out of sheer greed, the mass media have also been putting more emphasis on the dark (and hence exciting) side of American life.

As Whitman shows, liberals who want the government to do something about a social or economic problem instinctively assume that the best way to get action is to exaggerate the problem. Those who want to help the homeless, for example, have always exaggerated the number of people on the streets. Those who want to help crack babies, victims of domestic violence, or vanishing species do the same thing. Advocates who want a new or bigger program also assume they must portray this program as the solution to a new (or growing) problem. So even when teenage pregnancy and drug use are falling, advocates almost invariably suggest that they are becoming more common. In the short run, this strategy often works. Eventually, however, constant claims that a problem is getting worse may well convince the public that programs designed to solve the problem must have been ineffective or counterproductive.

When liberals tore their hair out about social problems in the 1960s, conservatives usually responded by saying that the problem was exaggerated. This was especially true of economic problems. When liberals worried about poverty, conservatives said that American poverty was nothing compared to poverty in the past or in other countries. When liberals said poor people couldn't find work, conservatives said that was because the poor were unwilling to take the jobs that were available. When liberals said poor children had little chance of escaping poverty, conservatives pointed to all the children of immigrants who had climbed into the middle class. This duet has been repeated many times over the past two decades. In the 1980s, for example, when liberals said several million people were homeless, conservatives argued (correctly) that the number was far smaller.

On social issues, however, conservatives have joined the apocalyptic camp, competing with liberals to publicize the decline and fall of practically everything. This has been the case with drug use, teenage motherhood, and conditions in inner-city schools, for example. Indeed, Whitman reports that those who call themselves Republicans have become more pessimistic about the nation's future than those who call themselves Democrats. The big difference between Republicans and Democrats is no longer that Republicans cannot abide criticism of their favorite country but that the Republicans blame national decline on liberal permissiveness and big government, whereas Democrats blame decline on conservative hard-heartedness and cutbacks in government programs.

The bipartisan consensus that the country is falling apart has encouraged the mass media to emphasize stories consistent with this theme. Bad news is never hard to find, and the media have always given it a lot of attention. But an earlier generation of network newscasters thought they also had an obligation to provide less exciting news about issues on which viewers needed information if they were to make sensible political judgments. As the networks have lost market share and television has become more competitive, this "paternalistic" ideal has given way to the marketing department's view that news should compete for ratings on the same basis as other programs. Competition over ratings has meant more sex and violence on both news and entertainment shows. As Whitman says, TV now portrays a terrifying world. If most Americans think the real world is like the world they see on TV, it is easy to see why they think the country is in deep trouble. It is also easy to see why they think themselves extremely fortunate—after all, the things they see on TV hardly ever happen to them.

While the left and right now agree that America is in trouble, they do not agree about the reasons. The left still sees poverty, joblessness, discrimination, and blocked opportunities as the ultimate causes of most social problems. Thus, if crime, drug use, or teen pregnancy appears to be more common, the left assumes that this must be because poverty, joblessness, and discrimination are getting worse. Whitman shows that this whole line of argument is mistaken. Drug use today is lower than it was in the 1970s, crime is down, and teenage births are less common. Poverty has not vanished, but neither has it gotten worse. Racism is still very much with us, but it is much less pervasive than it was a generation ago. The unemployment rate among black men is still double the rate among whites, but neither rate has increased systematically over the past quarter century.

Most conservatives see social problems as a product of individual rather than societal failure. Like liberals, they think crime, drug use, teen pregnancy, and other ills are becoming more common. But most conservatives blame these trends on the relaxation of moral standards, the spread of hedonism, and the collapse of self-control, rather than on increases in poverty, joblessness, and the like. Many conservatives link these character changes to the "decline of family values"—a phrase that seems to be code for the spread of single-parent families.

The Optimism Gap shows that conservatives are as likely as liberals to misread—or misremember—the past. Are schools and colleges really being overwhelmed by an epidemic of cheating? Perhaps, but the problem does not seem to be any more pervasive today that it was a generation ago. Have Americans stopped caring about their neighbors? Not if we judge by how much of their money they give to charity or how much time they spend doing volunteer work. Has religion lost influence? Not if we judge by the percentage of Americans who say they believe in God, the percentage who attend religious services every week, or the kinds of churches they join. America seems to be one of the most religious countries on earth—a fact that may help explain our extraordinary optimism about our personal situation.

Although most of the facts refute the claim that America is

on the skids, there is one realm, namely relations between men and women, where behavior has clearly changed and has had considerable economic, political, and social impact. The question is not whether change has occurred but whether it constitutes progress or retrogression. Liberals see most recent changes in relations between the sexes as progressive. Conservatives take a far gloomier view. Whitman does not discuss relationships between the sexes per se, but I am convinced that these changes in the makeup of families are a major reason why so many conservatives look back on the 1950s as America's golden age.

One big change is that more women, including mothers of very young children, work at least part-time. Until relatively recently, most cultural conservatives assumed that mothers who worked were neglecting their children in order to advance their career or raise their material standard of living. But with millions of mothers now in the labor force, it has become increasingly clear that their children are hard to distinguish from the children of full-time homemakers.[1] Meanwhile, many conservatives have convinced themselves that forcing single mothers to work will cut welfare spending and out-of-wedlock childbearing. Having taken that position, they find it harder to argue that encouraging mothers to work is bad for their children. So today working mothers are less likely to be denounced by conservatives than they were a decade or two ago. In practice, women are now more able to support themselves if their marriage breaks up, which has likely boosted the divorce rate and the number of single-parent households.

The second big change involves attitudes toward premarital sex. This shift has had a significant effect on how people perceive the nation's religious and social climate. Those who believe that premarital sex is always wrong still exert considerable political influence; but most Americans—including most teenagers—now seem to feel that whether they should engage in premarital sex is an emotional rather than a moral question.

Even those who remain virgins until they marry are reluctant to pass moral judgment on those who do not. This is not, of course, as much of a change as some people imagine. Even in the 1950s, many unmarried couples had sexual intercourse, especially if they were "going steady" and expected to marry at some point in the future. Nonetheless, today's teenagers report losing their virginity at a somewhat younger age than their parents did.[2] Perhaps equally important, far fewer young couples feel that they need a marriage license in order to be comfortable in bed with one another or make their relationship acceptable to others. As a result, couples are marrying much later than they once did.

The final shift in relations between the sexes is that more mothers are raising children without benefit of matrimony. Until the 1960s, social stigma made unwed motherhood rare, at least among whites. Any woman who had a baby out of wedlock had obviously been sleeping with someone to whom she was not married. Worse yet, she had been sleeping with someone whom she did not intend to marry—or who did not intend to marry her—even if she became pregnant. Separating sex from love in this way was the mark of a loose woman. Today, the very term, "loose woman," sounds anachronistic. This change in attitudes has led to a big decline in shotgun weddings. Premarital pregnancies have not declined, so the number of unwed mothers has soared.

Liberals seldom find the spread of single-parent families as alarming as conservatives do, but almost everyone finds the trend troubling. That said, it is still important to be clear that this change has produced winners as well as losers. No one has made a convincing case that mothers as a group would be better off if they were all required to spend their lives with the father of their first child, or that fathers would be better off if they had to spend their lives with the mother of their first child. Parents who divorce or decide not to marry make this choice with their eyes open, and they know a lot more about their prospective partners than we do.

The spread of single parenthood is, however, probably bad for children. Parents usually think they put their children's interests before their own, but in many cases they are fooling themselves. Single-parent families almost inevitably create greater economic hardships for their offspring. As Whitman notes in passing, children raised in single-parent families also fare worse than those raised in two-parent families on almost every objective yardstick, from behavioral problems and school achievement to adult success. This is partly because unwed and divorced mothers tend to have a multitude of other disadvantages, ranging from low school achievement to higher rates of depression, that would handicap their children even if the parents were married.

Although the spread of single parenthood almost certainly has had some adverse effects on children, this one trend hardly suffices to prove that the country as a whole is headed in the wrong direction. Plenty of terrible things are still happening in this country. But that has always been true. In politics, we always have to choose between imperfect alternatives. Big choices, like whether the government should keep trying to move the country in the same direction or somehow try to reverse course, are no exception to this rule. When we make such choices, we need all the objective evidence we can find to temper our emotional judgments and our tendency to nostalgia. *The Optimism Gap* does not cover every conceivable difference between today's society and the world that existed a generation ago, but it does cover almost all the most widely cited indicators of decline, and in almost every case it finds stability or improvement. That does not prove that America has been going in the right direction. But it does suggest that in almost every respect we can measure, turning back the clock would either leave things unchanged or make them worse.

We are left with the question of how to get this message across to disgruntled Americans who think things should be better than they are. The obvious answer is that we need to persuade politicians, advocacy groups, and journalists that exaggerating the nation's problems is both false and dangerous, like yelling "fire" in a crowded theater that is not in fact on fire. But selling this notion will be an uphill fight, because both advocacy groups and the mass media have found that peddling bad news is in their short-term interest, and there is no obvious way of making them take a longer view. *The Optimism Gap* should, however, become a bible for anyone who wants to rethink the conventional wisdom and adopt policies based on facts instead of myths.

Christopher Jencks,
The Malcolm Wiener Professor of Social Policy
John F. Kennedy School of Government,
Harvard University

I make frequent reference in *The Optimism Gap* to public opinion polls. Many readers rightfully distrust polls. They will wonder about the size, accuracy, and sturdiness of the survey results I cite in the text.

I share many of these concerns. The chief drawback to using polls to chart the reach of the I'm OK–They're Not syndrome is that people inevitably exaggerate their socially desirable behaviors when talking to pollsters and minimize their undesirable ones. Nonetheless, as I argue in more detail in chapter 3, I believe these poll results also genuinely mirror how people feel about themselves and their world. The I'm OK–They're Not syndrome is one of the most robust patterns in all of social psychology, and I know of no scholar who argues that the syndrome is a methodological artifact.

The public opinion results I cite are generally drawn from random surveys, usually done over the telephone, of 1,000 to 1,200 Americans. Most pollsters who seek to make their results "nationally representative" use sample sizes of 1,000 individuals.

Since pollsters do not interview everyone in the nation, virtually all surveys are subject to sampling error. Nonetheless, poll results can be representative of the thinking of the public at large, as long as the wording and order of the questions do not introduce a bias, the response rate of people contacted to be interviewed is high, and the identity of the questioner does not skew the results. For polls of 1,000 people, the sample error is plus or minus 2 to 3 percentage points at the 95 percent confidence level—meaning that if the same poll was done repeatedly, the odds are that 95 percent of the time the results would fall within 2 to 3 percentage points of the original poll finding. In cases where I cite poll results from surveys of conspicuously more or fewer people than 1,000, I generally cite the sample size in the text.

Journalists and members of the public often complain that statistics lie. But that conclusion is a lazy man's critique. Statistics can also show the truth—in a way that personal observation and hunches cannot. That is why I use polling data, despite its flaws.

ACKNOWLEDGMENTS

L ike many authors, I sometimes wondered whether this book would ever meet the bookbinder. Its publication owes much to a handful of individuals—both those who had faith in what I was saying and those who thought I was wrong.

At *U.S. News & World Report*, Lee Rainie sought for more than a year to have the magazine publish an article-length version of this book, which appeared under the headline "I'm OK, You're Not" in the magazine's December 16, 1996, issue. Without Lee's support, the article and this book would never have been commissioned. Mike Ruby, the former editor of *U.S. News*, was one of those who thought I was wrong, though he unwaveringly supported every other article I wrote for *U.S. News* during his long tenure at the magazine. His criticism forced me to rethink and clarify sections of the original magazine article.

I am grateful, too, to Jim Fallows, the editor of *U.S. News & World Report* who published the "I'm OK, You're Not" article, and for his support of the leave I required to finish this book. Lincoln Caplan edited the *U.S. News* story and graciously but persistently pushed me to expand the article into a book. Christopher Jencks at the John F. Kennedy School of Government at Harvard University also provided encouragement to press ahead on several occasions when my enthusiasm had waned. I am indebted to him for contributing a foreword to *The Optimism Gap* and a meticulous critique of the manuscript.

At Walker and Company, my publisher, George Gibson,

believed in this book immediately and stuck with it. I thank him for his faith and appreciate his decency and integrity. Despite my initial skepticism, my editor at Walker, Jackie Johnson, ingeniously reshuffled several sections of the manuscript and added some deft line editing. At *U.S. News,* the librarians provided their customary superb research support, no matter how many times I sent them in search of another obscurity.

Last, but of course not least, I want to thank my wife, Lynn Rosellini, who shouldered the lion's share of the care of our spirited daughter, Lily, while I was finishing this book. Lynn is the best editor a writer could have. I feel lucky that she is my soul mate, too.

Much of what everyone "knows" about the state of our nation is wrong. A large majority of Americans now believe that the nation is in decline. The causes of this decline are both familiar and disputed. Conservatives blame family breakdown, crime, and spiritual sloth for our national atrophy. Liberals attribute the decline to the forces of modern-day capitalism, racism, and greed; the poor and the working-class stiffs in the factories can no longer get ahead the way they once did, or so the argument goes. Yet while liberals and conservatives disagree about first causes, they nonetheless agree that the nation, like Rome before the fall, has already been compromised. The American Dream is now endangered.

Beneath this glum appraisal, however, lies a paradox. While most Americans attest to the country's deterioration, they are equally adamant that they and their families are, on the whole, flourishing. This optimism gap[1]—the gulf between people's upbeat assessment of their personal lives and their downbeat assessment of the country and its public institutions—helps explain much of the nation's current political paralysis.

Close to hearth and home, Americans nowadays think social ills aren't all that applicable to them or their family. This private optimism prompts voters to underestimate the seriousness of problems in their own communities and saps attempts to fix troubled local institutions—for example, an inferior public school, a halfhearted community watch program, or a festering pollution problem. Farther from home, however, problems like drug abuse or family breakdown seem too global or intractable to do much about. Ironically, this public pessimism has much the same effect as people's private optimism: It undermines lawmakers and reform-minded voters who wish to attack social problems, such as soaring health care costs, child abuse, and housing discrimination. Not all that long ago, personal experience and public understanding were more intimately linked. Today, Americans tend to misconstrue reality. They exaggerate the threats facing society and minimize the threats to themselves. Their distorted view of "others" and the society around them leads them to distrust institutions more than ever, even as they feel less compunction to act on behalf of the commonweal.

This national gloom, the sense of living in Babylon, is fairly new. To be sure, America has always had a hefty number of naysayers, particularly among the intellectual elite and the press. The country has also endured periodic times of tragedy and hardship. Prior to the 1990s, however, Americans typically were optimistic about not only their personal prospects but those of their children's generation. Republican pollster Frank Luntz reported in 1995 that "the belief that the next generation could be worse off than the present one was foreign to America. Until now."[2] Only one in three Americans thought that future generations would enjoy a better standard of living or quality of life than their parents had at the same age. That figure, Luntz noted, "is the lowest recorded reading for this statistic since scientific polling began in the 1930s."[3]

The Gallup poll shows much the same optimism gap, only in an international perspective. In 1995, Gallup asked the residents of 17 nations how satisfied or dissatisfied they were with how things were going with their personal lives. It also queried people as to whether they thought the world today was better or worse than in the past and how it would fare in the future.

U.S. citizens turned out to be among the most optimistic

in the world about their own lives—83 percent reported being satisfied.⁴ But they were more pessimistic than citizens from most other nations about how the present compared with the past or future. Three in five Americans said the next generation of children would live in a worse world. Just over half said the world today was worse than in their parents' day. In fact, out of the 17 nations, in only one country (Venezuela) were residents more likely than U.S. residents to think the world they lived in today was worse off than in their parents' time.⁵

As an adolescent in the late 1960s, I heard a very different debate about America in class and at the dinner table. I attended a liberal Quaker high school in a gritty Philadelphia neighborhood on Germantown Avenue, the same street that General Colin Powell, President Bill Clinton, and various dignitaries helped clean during the 1997 summit on volunteerism. When I was a student, the school was rife with social protest. Yet despite the racial tumult of the era, despite the doubts about America's involvement in Vietnam and about capitalism itself, there was little sense at the time that our days of national progress were numbered.

At home, the character of the conversation about the country was much the same. My mother and members of her extended family successfully fled the Holocaust; my parents hardly could be considered naive about a society's capacity for evil and regression. They expressed plenty of doubts about whether America and Western civilization had steadily improved, and believed that society sometimes regressed before inching forward. But I do not recall them saying that they wished they could go back to the days of the 1940s or 1950s, or presuming that America was somehow doomed to slide downhill in decades to come.

As late as 1960, Henry Luce, editor in chief of *Life* magazine, sponsored a forum in his magazine that featured national leaders and thinkers answering the questions "What now shall

Americans *do* with the greatness of their nation? And is it great enough?"[6] It is hard to envision *Life,* or any other national newsmagazine, sponsoring a similar forum in 1998 premised on the notion of American progress. The shift between the two eras is so complete, the notion of decline so omnipresent, that voters now take the idea of national deterioration almost as a given.

For their 1996 book *The State of Disunion,* James Davison Hunter and Carl Bowman had the Gallup Organization survey more than 2,000 adults face-to-face about the status of the country, with each interview lasting an average of an hour and a half. To paraphrase an old Turkish legend, they found all is ruin, a veritable portrait gallery of decay. More than half of those surveyed thought the quality of the schools had declined, along with people's family life and standard of living, the American work ethic, and our moral and ethical standards. Most people also believed that crime and public safety, the health care system, the quality of national leaders, and the honesty and integrity of the average American had all deteriorated, too. About a quarter to a third of those surveyed said that conditions had held steady in these areas of American life. But only a small minority—generally less than 15 percent—admitted to seeing *any* improvement.[7]

It is particularly odd that Americans feel so forlorn about their country in 1998. At a time when the Soviet Union has dissolved, the Berlin Wall has crumbled, far-reaching peace agreements have been signed in the Mideast, the nuclear arms race has essentially ended, unemployment is at its lowest rate in a quarter century, consumer confidence is the highest it's been in 28 years, more people own homes than ever before, material affluence and longevity are unprecedented, and crime has plummeted, Americans still display fear and loathing about the state of the nation. The threats that have dominated American life for almost half a century have either vanished or receded. Yet there is little celebration in Mudville.

Imagine how worried voters would be if the economy were in a recession, the arms race were racing ahead, violent crime were rising, and people's standards of living were dropping. Or if the country were engaged in a major war. "In this world there are only two tragedies," Oscar Wilde one wrote. "One is not getting what one wants, and the other is getting it."[8] America's "tragedy," it would seem, is that the nation has been touched one too many times by the hand of success.

The Compared-to-What Test

"Life is hard," someone once remarked to Voltaire, who retorted, "Compared to what?"[9] The tag line "Compared to what?" later became the title and refrain of a song by jazz great Les McCann. It is the same refrain that politicians and pundits routinely ignore when decrying the decline of America.

It almost goes without saying that progress or decline can only be demonstrated with a benchmark of comparison. The very definition of progress suggests moving forward from a "worse" point in the past to a "better" point in the present. The question of whether the nation has regressed or advanced in some respect can be resolved only by comparing the situation today with the situation previously. All this sounds obvious. But many journalists, academics, and voters base their conviction that America is coming apart on little more than their personal opinion or gut feelings.

Sometimes the declinists use such nebulous language that there is no way to agree or disagree with their claims. In his 1996 book *We Know What to Do,* former Secretary of Education Lamar Alexander writes, "The nation is clearly off track . . . no one remembers when we were so out of sorts."[10] Alexander's comment may or may not be accurate—in every era, after all, some people claim to feel "out of sorts." Harvard professor Cornel West meanwhile claims that American society has led to "the collapse of meaning in life. . . . We have created rootless, dangling people."[11] But people may have felt that they lived in societies filled with rootless and dangling people in the past, too. One could just as readily assert that we live in a society of gibberish and blatherskites. Almost as vague are claims of "spiritual decline" or "moral decline." Are people less likely today to say they believe in God? Are they more likely to cheat on their taxes? To lie? Those are better indicators of moral progress or retrenchment.

In the course of writing this book, I consistently encountered three rhetorical devices that people rely on to herald American decline. The first is a kind of argument-by-anecdote. The evening news will feature some powerful story that seems unprecedented—say, two parents go on vacation and leave their kids "home alone." This story confirms to the viewers that parents care less about children today than they did in the past.

In fact, the segment may well have been misleading. The evening news may have failed to document that this type of incident occurs rarely, or that the broader problems of latchkey kids today pale beside those of the country's urchins in the early decades of this century, when tens of thousands of parents put children in orphanages, left babies on doorsteps, or hired them out as child labor.

The second device is to lower the ante of what constitutes a problem or crisis. Two decades ago, economist John Kenneth Galbraith joked that every book publisher encouraged an author to call his or her book *The Crisis of American Democracy* to boost sales.[12] A favorite turn of phrase among politicians, advocates, and pundits today is to talk about the "quiet crisis" in some aspect of national life. In the fall of 1996, President Clinton said the nation's child support system was having a "quiet crisis,"[13] and Richard Gephardt, the House minority leader, has said the same for the American family.[14] (Politicians similarly define down the meaning of a "major war" and "global conflict" to hype the dangers of what are comparatively modest, regional conflicts.)[15]

One consequence of this definition-creep is that a segment of the electorate *never* thinks the country is in a period of robust progress. Most Americans now think of the 1950s as the good ol' days, an era when everything was more or less right in the nation. They conveniently forget the Korean War, the segregated South, McCarthyism, the arms race and the bomb shelter drills, and the deadly polio epidemics. At the time, though, not everyone thought things were so wonderful. The basic conundrum, as John Mueller, professor of political science at the University of Rochester, has pointed out, is that "no matter how much better the present gets, the past gets better faster in reflection, and we are, accordingly, always notably worse off than we used to be. Golden ages, thus, do happen, but we are never actually *in* them."[16]

The third rhetorical device for heralding decline is exaggeration. It is the trickiest of the lot, because it contains a kernel of truth. Some declinists argue, in effect, that if a few social problems are worse today than at some earlier point in American history, then life today must be worse *as a whole* than in the past. Compared to the 1950s, there is more crime today and children are more likely to grow up in single-parent households.

Both crime and family breakdown are important signs of change for the worse. But two measures are not enough to show that Americans had it better in the 1950s than today. That kind of assessment requires one to look far more thoroughly at how life has changed in the half century. Has the standard of living risen? Do people live longer? Are they healthier while they are alive? Is there more opportunity today than in the past, especially for minorities and women, and less poverty? How do Americans feel about their ties to family and work, compared to the past? How does education today compare with that provided in earlier eras? Do people seem more or less ethical and spiritual? What kind of provision is made for the elderly? And so on.

Deciding whether the nation is making progress or declining is tricky. One must weigh the inevitably imperfect evidence as best as possible and make judgments about which goals are most central to the American Dream, as I seek to do in several chapters of *The Optimism Gap*. I believe most readers will conclude that the nation is in a period of progress, not retrogression. At minimum, it is clear that both liberal and conservative claims about American decline are wildly exaggerated.

The Revisionists

In the latter half of the 1990s, a handful of journalists and scholars have examined how the present stacks up against the past in quantitative terms. They, too, have concluded that America, in most instances, has made substantial progress in recent decades. *The State of the Nation* by Harvard president emeritus Derek Bok, *The State of Humanity,* edited by Julian L. Simon, and *The New American Reality* by Reynolds Farley all provide thorough analyses of the state of the nation today. *Newsweek* columnist Robert Samuelson's provocative 1995 book, *The Good Life and Its Discontents,* also forcefully makes the case that Americans have flourished in the post-1945 era.[17]

The Optimism Gap differs from these earlier analyses in several respects. Robert Samuelson compares America today and at the end of World War II, while Derek Bok compares the nation in 1995 and 1960. The contributors to Julian L. Simon's tome take an even longer, more academic view, often tracking human progress over several centuries. Unlike these authors, I have chosen 1970 and the present day as my two benchmarks. (In several cases, such as drug use by high school seniors, no data are available until the mid-1970s. In these cases I use the first available point of comparison.)

I have chosen to concentrate on progress over the last quarter century for two reasons. First, that time period roughly corresponds with the onset of a new generation. When Americans say the present generation is worse off than the previous one, they typically are referring to individuals who grew up 20 to 30 years ago, not 50 years ago. Second, I look chiefly at the post-1970 record because that time frame presents the strongest case for American decline.

For conservatives, comparing the postwar years to the present is potentially misleading because it can confound the advances of the 1950s and early 1960s with the deterioration that allegedly followed in later years. To those on the left who believe the country has declined economically, longer comparisons are also problematic. They date the deterioration of the American working class to 1973 and the disastrous Arab oil embargo.

To minimize questions about ideological motive, I have tried, where possible, to rely on research by conservatives to debunk right-wing claims of decline, and research by liberals to debunk similar claims from those on the left. I chose not to compare economic and social conditions in the United States to those of other nations. When assessing whether life has changed for better or worse, most Americans are much more likely to compare themselves to their immediate predecessors than to our contemporaries in, say, Scandinavia.[18]

Despite the generally upbeat conclusions of Bok, Samuelson, and Simon, they all grappled with a basic paradox about American progress. As political scientist Aaron Wildavsky once put it, how can one explain the fact that people are "doing better but feeling worse" about society?[19] Each author cites some common villains to explain this conundrum: Hyped news coverage makes people think matters are worse than they really are, the revolution of rising expectations leaves people unhappy even as they prosper, and so on.

The optimism gap provides a means for explaining and

understanding the paradox. People are feeling better about their own lives but feel that "other" Americans in the society at large are doing poorly. I do not agree with some revisionist critics that America has become a nation of whiners, or that voters' current sense of malaise stems from boredom. There are compelling reasons, as I point out in this book, why even rational and sophisticated individuals believe this skewed picture is accurate.

The optimism gap, also known as the I'm OK–They're Not syndrome, has become far more ingrained and powerful in the last quarter century. It has, to use a German term, become a *Weltanschauung,* a comprehensive way of seeing and judging the world. The spread of this phenomenon is not the only explanation for the predicament that Americans find themselves in. But it should be a central part of any such explanation. To date, the public, the press, and politicians have largely ignored the consequences of this split vision.

In some sense I am an odd person to write a book that, on the whole, is quite optimistic about the country. For the last 13 years I've been a reporter for *U.S. News & World Report* covering the disadvantaged. By nature I'm not an optimist, and my reporting has given me abundant opportunity to exercise my skepticism. I've interviewed prisoners with AIDS, homeless alcoholics, chronic welfare recipients, illegal immigrants, residents of white slums and black ghettos, pregnant teenagers, the children of crack addicts—the list could go on and on. A fellow reporter at *U.S. News* once joked that every story I wrote on social policy could be summed up by a two-word theme: "Nothing works."

I wrote this book in part because I have concluded that the country, and the press in particular, has too many cynics. I believe that the distinction people draw between "we" and "they" is neither correct nor necessarily inevitable. It is a dividing line that is exaggerated at best and pernicious at worst. Historian Arthur Schlesinger, Jr., has written that the We-They syndrome has "caused more dominating, fearing, hating, killing than any other single cause since time began."[20] Today, the We-They syndrome may not be leading America into war or a costly international jihad. But it is deterring voters and politicians alike from tackling the nation's social ills. And it is furtively diminishing both "them" and "us."

The New Pandora's Box

CHAPTER ONE

Every man is a good man in a bad world—as he himself knows.

WILLIAM SAROYAN[1]

If you are like most Americans, you think you are a better-than-average driver. You believe your job and home life stack up pretty well against those of the typical Joe or Jane. Asked to compare yourself with other citizens, you would likely conclude that your doctors generally provide superior care, the local school outperforms most public schools, your drinking water and air are clean enough, and the block you live on is not crime ridden.[2]

But if you think like most Americans, you also believe that much of the rest of the country is going to hell. Beyond your immediate family and neighborhood, you see a nation where the economy is uneven and public schools have become mediocre or worse; religion is no longer valued; family breakdown is pandemic; the health care system is out of control; pollution befouls cities; and a new wave of violent crime is rampant.[3]

A psychologist might dub this split-screen perception as cognitive dissonance: You feel the country is foundering, yet you are reasonably content with your own personal situation. This I'm OK–They're Not syndrome or optimism gap is pervasive, shared by more than half the populace, over 100 million fellow

Americans. Poll after poll now discloses that the American voter is metaphorically peeking out of Pandora's box into a world filled with all the human ills. Yet inside the box, one human blessing—hope, or the force of personal optimism—persists. As NBC news anchor Tom Brokaw has put it: "If America today were a country-and-western song, its title might be 'If I'm Doin' So Good, Why Am I Feelin' So Bad?' That is the essential dilemma as we approach the millennium."[4]

Social science researchers first started measuring the optimism gap almost 40 years ago. In 1959, pollsters asked Americans to rate their own condition and that of the nation on a 1 to 10 scale. According to a Pew Research Center survey taken shortly after the 1996 election, the gap between people's assessment of their own future and their evaluation of the country's future was unprecedented, as the accompanying graph depicts.

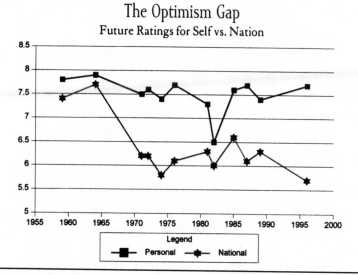

The Optimism Gap
Future Ratings for Self vs. Nation

SOURCE: From "The Optimism Gap Grows—Politics, Morality, Entitlements Sap Confidence," The Pew Research Center for the People & the Press

Personal optimism is currently at near record levels.[5] The 1997 edition of the Harris poll's "Feel Good" index—which asks

American adults what they feel good about—found that 90 percent or more of the public felt good about their relations with their families, their homes, and the quality of their lives. More than 80 percent were upbeat about their standard of living and their health, and 79 percent said they felt good about the city, town, or county in which they lived. In their own communities, two out of three adults even felt good about their fellow residents' morals and values. But Americans don't think well of other communities or the country at large.[6]

As Humphrey Taylor, chairman of Louis Harris and Associates, wrote in explaining the poll results, "It is as though there are two different countries, the one people know personally which they are happy with, and the one they see on television and read about in the newspapers which they think is in bad shape."[7] Over 60 percent of respondents in the Harris poll said they did not feel good about the morals and values of Americans in general, and slightly more than half said they did not feel good about the nation's economy.[8]

Today, public pessimism about the future is especially marked. As the graph from the Pew survey shows, people's pessimism about where the United States will stand five years from now even slightly surpasses the previous doom-and-gloom peak of April 1974—when the nation was in the throes of the Watergate scandal, the end of the Vietnam War, and the oil crisis.

Routinely, politicians, pundits, and pollsters describe today's voters as angry and disillusioned. That assessment, however, misses half of the story. The high mark of media coverage about voter anger occurred around the 1994 election, when the Republicans took over both houses of Congress. In a poll taken shortly before the 1994 election, GOP strategist Frank Luntz asked members of the public if they felt "things in America [were] headed in the right direction or . . . [were] pretty seriously off on the wrong track?" In keeping with the angry-voter stories, 60 percent of Americans said the country was on the wrong track. However, when Luntz asked people if things in their *own* lives and family were going well, the perceptions flipped. Almost 90 percent said they personally were on the right track.[9] Even the "angry white male," the poster boy of the 1994 election, turned out to be quite content with matters in his own life. Roughly 70 percent of white males said they personally had achieved or were close to fulfilling their vision of the American Dream; about 70 percent said they were satisfied with their current job; and more than 80 percent affirmed they were optimistic about their own future.[10]

This "us" versus "them" worldview is "the most important *and* least comprehended aspect of public opinion," says Ed Goeas, another GOP pollster. "It is hard to fathom the mood of the country or the fate of government policies unless you understand this split vision."[11]

Ultimately, that split vision has two overarching consequences: The first is that voters exaggerate national problems and doubt the country's ability—especially the government's ability—to help solve them. The second is that taxpayers understate problems in their own backyard and cannot be roused to address them. Both consequences breed a kind of paralysis in civic life. Chester Finn, Jr., a former Reagan administration appointee, calls the I'm OK–They're Not syndrome "a recipe for stasis. It makes for a very conservative nation—in the worst sense of the word. It makes for complacency."[12]

The I'm OK–They're Not syndrome undergirds many of the seemingly contradictory positions voters have taken on some of the leading issues of the day. The syndrome helps explain why taxpayers can decry public schools as blackboard jungles but are convinced they don't need to fix their own child's school[13] or why city dwellers deplore the spread of violent crime but fail to turn on their own back porch lights at night as a security measure.[14] It helps explain why Americans think other people are failing to save enough for retirement, but they themselves don't need to boost their savings and expect to live out their golden years in comfort.[15] And it helps elucidate why tax-payers favor paring back the federal government and balancing the budget yet think this can be accomplished without trimming programs that might one day benefit their family or themselves, including Social Security, Medicare, Medicaid, unemployment insurance, environmental spending, law enforcement, and college student loans.[16]

This optimism gap handcuffs Democratic and Republican policymakers alike. When Lamar Alexander, a 1996 Republican presidential candidate, served as secretary of education, he fumed regularly about parents who were overly satisfied with their local school. In a 1991 speech, Alexander called the I'm OK–They're Not syndrome "the overwhelming obstacle to everything we are trying to do. Too many [people] say, 'well, the nation may be at risk, but I'm okay. Schools are bad, but my school is good. Sorry to hear about the [national results of the eighth grade] math [achievement] test[s], but my Johnnie is doing fine.' "[17]

On the political left, First Lady Hillary Rodham Clinton contends that the optimism gap undermines government efforts to aid children and the resolve of parents to confront their own family problems. In a syndicated column several years ago, she observed that "the guilt many Americans feel about their own children—because of longer work hours, divorce and shrinking resources—is often projected as anger onto other people's children. But there is no such thing as 'other people's children.' "[18] Chester Finn, Jr., now with the Hudson Institute, sums up by saying that the "fundamental problem is that voters—even when they believe the world is going to hell in a handbasket—are so unwilling to alter their own lives."[19]

The Schools: Not My Johnny

One almost universal prescription for raising student achievement is to boost parental involvement at school and at home.

Recent national legislation, such as the Goals 2000 law, has made the expansion and strengthening of parental involvement programs an explicit priority. Elementary and secondary schools, for example, must earmark money for school-family programs or risk losing federal funds.[20] Yet school officials know surprisingly little about how to encourage effective parental involvement in any organized way.

The John Hanson Middle School in Waldorf, Maryland, is a drab gray-and-white modern edifice nestled amid playing fields and farmland, a quintessential suburban school. Located 22 miles from Washington, the town of Waldorf is home to 15,000 residents and has fast-food restaurants, shopping malls, industrial parks, and a few quirky landmarks. The John Hanson school is named after a local Revolutionary War–era patriot who was the first president of the U.S. Congress under the Articles of Confederation. Hanson is sometimes grandly described by locals as "the first president of the United States." Inside the central entrance to the school is a large banner that greets students with the admonition: "People Who Know Say No to Drugs." The asphalt parking lot outside the entrance is dotted with signs that declare the school to be a tobacco-free and drug-free zone.

John Hanson is an unexceptional school, and that is one reason the tale of parental involvement there is so revealing. In the 1993–94 school year, John Hanson students tested below state averages on Maryland's rigorous achievement test. They ranked near or at the bottom of middle schools in its region, Charles County.[21] Yet no group of parents ever brought up the students' mediocre test scores at a PTA meeting or discussed the school's undistinguished academic record with the school's principal.[22] The following year a school redistricting reduced overcrowding at the school. Test scores went up, so that John Hanson scores exceeded county averages but still remained below the statewide average. In the 1996–97 school year, John Hanson test scores remained below the state averages.[23]

However, most parents at John Hanson had no idea how the school compared with nearby schools then or now. Karla Schlaefli, chair of the school PTSA (Parent-Teacher-Student Association) in the 1994–95 school year, reported that her own daughter did well at John Hanson and that she herself heard few accounts of parental dissatisfaction. "As long as there isn't a horrible problem in the school," said Schlaefli, "most parents aren't going to be real vocal. They don't nose around too much if they think everything is OK with the system."[24]

The pattern of parental involvement at John Hanson is much like that at thousands of other schools where everything seems more or less "OK"—a pattern that has all the ingredients of Chester Finn's "recipe for stasis." A core group of a dozen or so parents are regularly involved in arranging school activities such as a skate night at the local roller rink, and providing chaperones for a school dance or field trip. But the vast majority of parents rarely call teachers to discuss their children's progress or visit the middle school, unless there is a special event in which their child participates, like a winter concert.

During the 1994–95 school year, John Hanson had more than 1,000 students enrolled, but the PTSA had about 175 members. At most board meetings, which were open to PTSA members, perhaps 25 people showed up, and when the PTSA held a meeting to elect officers for the upcoming school year, only about a dozen parents attended. Yet the PTSA at John Hanson was one of the *more* active PTSAs in the county, and Garth Bowling, the school's well-regarded principal, has repeatedly encouraged parents to visit the school and participate in volunteer activities and school administration. Cindy Petrecca, the president of the Charles County council of PTAs, said that "you would think that there would be more of a parental uprising over low test scores than over dress codes, but that's not the case. When the schools started enforcing dress codes and the kids complained to their parents—that's what the principals and teachers would hear about."[25]

Consistent with Petrecca's experience, parents who have participated in national polls consistently think the schools their children attend provide good to excellent educations (though, if they could afford them, some parents would prefer to send their children to private schools).[26] In the annual Gallup poll for *Phi Delta Kappan* in 1996, 66 percent of public school parents said they would give the school their oldest child attends a grade of A or B overall, but only 21 percent gave the nation's public schools an A or B. Parents were quite specific about the ways in which they thought their local public school outstripped other schools. Roughly two-thirds of the parents who thought the local public school superior felt it had less crime and violence, fewer racial disturbances, better discipline, and superior teachers, and placed more emphasis on academic achievement than other public schools.[27]

Moreover, parents think well of their own involvement with their child's school. "Most people," as Lamar Alexander puts it, "don't think we have a problem."[28] Polls show that parents believe the support shown by other parents at their child's school is reasonably high, and that their own parenting skills and involvement in school activities easily surpass those of their own parents.[29] Yet a hefty majority of parents are also convinced that most parents of children at *other* schools neglect their responsibilities in educating their kids—help out too little with homework, leave their children alone too much after school, and fail to discipline them.[30]

Most adults, including those without children, echo such sentiments. A survey of some 2,000 adults in 1997 by the *Wall Street Journal* and NBC News found that when Americans think about "what will set the schools right . . . they don't hesitate to give an answer: parents. Parents, straightening out their unruly children. Parents, holding the family together. Parents, setting a good example. . . . The irony is that parents insist they are involved with their children's school—that it's everyone else who isn't. Most of those surveyed said they read aloud to their children, help them with homework, and attend parent-teacher conferences."[31]

The tenacity of this it's-thee-not-me outlook can be startling. It cuts across class lines. Nationally, poor families and families on welfare rank their local schools just as highly as middle-class families do.[32] And even in large cities like New York, Houston, and Chicago, where many of the public schools are plainly faltering, parents think well of their local public schools.[33]

Consider the case of Chicago. In 1987, then–Secretary of Education William Bennett cited Chicago as his top candidate for the "worst" public school system in the nation. High school seniors there posted abysmal test scores, and city schools had a dropout rate in excess of 40 percent. "How can anyone who feels about children not feel terrible about Chicago schools?" Bennett asked rhetorically. "You have an educational meltdown."[34]

The following year, the state legislature passed a radical reform law that created local councils at every Chicago school. The councils were effectively dominated by six elected parents, who had the power to hire and fire principals and exercised substantial control over state educational funds previously routed through a central bureaucracy. Reports at the time portrayed parents as in a rage worthy of Howard Beale in the movie *Network:* One study said "people were mad as hell" and "parents were desperate."[35]

A funny thing happened, though, on the way to the reform. Parents, it turned out, were chiefly mad about other people's schools, not the schools their own children attended. A survey of white, black, and Hispanic public school parents, the results of which are summarized in Dan Lewis and Kathryn Nakagawa's 1995 book *Race and Educational Reform in the American Metropolis,* showed that "in the eyes of the parents, the Chicago public schools are adequately educating their children."[36] Coauthor Lewis marveled that "80 percent of parents in Chicago are satisfied with their kid's school even when the public school system is a disaster on wheels."[37] The survey disclosed that more than 75 percent of the public school parents were somewhat or very satisfied with their child's school overall, with the quality of teaching, with time spent on reading and math, with discipline, and with information provided by the school for parents.[38]

Ironically, the issue that parents singled out as posing either a big problem or somewhat of a problem in the public schools was "lack of parental involvement." Sixty percent of parents singled out other parents for criticism. By contrast, fewer than half of all parents cited poor achievement, high dropout rates, gang violence, or drugs as significant problems.[39] Parents, it seems, generally favor school reform. But they seem to doubt that their Johnny is much in need of it.

Electoral Politics and the Optimism Gap

In recent years, the optimism gap has played an important if often overlooked role in presidential campaigns, especially in President Clinton's reelection. On the advice of his pollsters, Clinton deliberately sought during 1996 to narrow the chasm between voters' favorable views of their own lives and their dismal perceptions of where the country and economy were headed. In the fall of 1995, when the media were full of gloom about corporate downsizing and declining wages, Clinton pollster Mark Penn noticed an oddity: Consumer confidence was at a 10-year high.[40] In a memo to Clinton's advisers, Penn warned that the "failure to recognize the optimism in the electorate and to correctly revive it . . . could be the single biggest mistake that we would make that would cost us the election."[41]

Clinton didn't make that mistake. He stopped talking about people being in a "funk."[42] Instead he championed good news about the economy and other social trends. By the time of the election, polls indicated that anywhere from 39 to 53 percent of voters thought the nation was headed in the right direction. A little more than half thought the same about the economy.[43] Those numbers may not sound like cause for jubilation, but they are far sunnier appraisals than voters had offered earlier in Clinton's first term. And as Penn predicted, voters optimistic about the state of the country turned out in massive numbers for Clinton.[44]

Despite Clinton's winning strategy, there are obviously important exceptions to the I'm OK–They're Not syndrome. Not everyone thinks things are "OK" in their private lives, nor has everyone become complacent; plenty of Americans struggle to overcome their financial and personal predicaments. The fact that many Americans believe the grass is actually browner in other people's backyards also leads them to worry that the problems afflicting their fellow citizens may soon invade their lives. "What makes people insecure," President Clinton has observed, "is when they feel like they're lost in the fun house. They're in a room where something can hit them from any direction at any time."[45] Polls show that roughly four in five Americans say they have not recently had a problem paying the mortgage, nor have financial constraints forced them to put off medical care or give up plans to attend college. Yet those same surveys disclose that almost half the voters are very concerned that *one day* they will not have enough money to cover their family's medical bills, tuition fees, or retirement costs.[46]

Some of the electorate's cynicism about the federal bureaucracy and other public institutions is justified, too. There are many social problems the government cannot solve. And over the years, bureaucratic programs have wasted their share of taxpayer dollars. Even so, the vast majority of Americans presently retain a deep-seated disconnect between their personal experiences and their evaluations of government. In 1996, for example, roughly half of the public disapproved of the job Congress was doing, yet more than 60 percent approved of their own congressional representative.[47]

The point is not that one's attitudes and personal experiences must necessarily comport with the average citizen's; obviously they often don't. The problem rather is that most of the electorate makes the opposite presumption: that is, my experience must be unlike other people's.

In private, some politicians and pollsters gripe that the I'm OK–They're Not syndrome shows how selfish and narcissistic Americans have become. However, that critique presumes that voters are being disingenuous when they say they are OK but others aren't. If, instead, voters do believe that crime is rising, scholastic achievement is falling, religion and morality are fading, living standards are declining, and the federal government wastes most of each dollar it spends—then many of the taxpayers' seemingly self-serving stances make sense.

Take the example of health care reform. Surveys show that 70 to 80 percent of the public believe that their own doctors provide them with quality medical care.[48] To cut costs, most voters think it is not necessary to place limits on their own health care coverage or that of the average American. A majority of the electorate believes the health care cost explosion could be halted by cutting out profit taking, fraud, and waste, chiefly by other people's doctors and ambulance-chasing lawyers.[49] The public's calculation is almost surely wrong; the aging of the population and the high costs of new medical technologies are likely the chief culprits behind high health care costs. But its position is not irrational. "People always nod if you tell them the public is selfish or stupid—it's the country's favorite indoor sport," says

Professor John Immerwahr, a researcher with the polling firm The Public Agenda. "There is a kind of logical consistency to the public's views that elected officials dismiss at their peril."[50]

The Me-First Test: The Unraveling of Health Care Reform

Typically, the optimism gap stifles public officials who are trying to rouse the public to redress a problem. It creates a kind of self-fulfilling prophecy: People's bleak view of the world leads them to conclude that not much can be done about some social problem; unaddressed, the problem then gets worse; this only confirms people's initial cynicism about the huge scale of the problem and the futility of reform.

On occasion, however, voters' gloomy prognosis of the world outside their communities seems to have the opposite effect. Their fears prod them into taking steps they might otherwise not have taken—as was the case with health care reform. The fact that roughly 90 percent of Americans felt the health care system was "in crisis"[51] when the Clinton administration took office provided much of the political impetus that helped launch the administration's health care plan.

In that sense, health care reform was what Gallup researcher David Moore called a "civic issue."[52] Taxpayers initially seemed to favor reform because they thought the country would be better off as a result, not because they themselves would benefit. The problem, however, is that the voters' commitment to such civic issues is shallow. Before long, the fact that people themselves feel "OK" saps their sense of urgency. Ultimately, the I'm OK–They're Not syndrome helped launch the Clinton administration's health care plan and then, in a bizarre twist, helped doom it.

When Bill Clinton announced his health care plan in September 1993, about 60 percent of the electorate supported it.[53] But in the months to come, surveys and focus group research tracked a dramatic reversal in public attitudes. Undoubtedly, the health care legislation failed to pass Congress for many reasons. But one survey of Republican and Democratic members of Congress by the Columbia Institute found that lawmakers themselves believed public opinion was the single greatest influence on the legislative debate. Asked to anonymously rate factors that mattered a "great deal" to the outcome of the debate, lawmakers were 10 times more likely to cite public opinion than to mention contributions from political action committees (PACs).[54]

Several Democratic leaders and numerous journalists attributed the demise of the Clinton health care plan to the famous "Harry and Louise" television commercials. Funded by the Health Insurance Association of America, they featured an actor and actress who claimed that Clinton's legislation would limit their health care choices and might bankrupt their own health care plan. While the ads ran only on CNN and on a few local stations, the press wrote and spoke about them numerous times. But comparatively few Americans actually saw the ads, since they never appeared on network television.[55] Even for people who did see the ads, they turned out to be ineffective and unmemorable. Most viewers, after seeing two of the ads, had no idea who Harry and Louise were, and couldn't recall the message of the ads an hour later.[56]

What did spur the shift in public opinion? "The death knell of the Clinton health care bill," suggests Robert Blendon of the Harvard School of Public Health, "was that the public came to perceive the plan as potentially making their personal circumstances worse."[57] By April 1994, polls showed that fewer than 20 percent of Americans believed Clinton's health plan would leave them better off personally, give them more choices of doctors, or decrease the amount they paid for medical care and health insurance. Just 6 percent of the public thought that the plan provided too little government involvement.[58]

A fair case, based on substantive objections, could have

been made for opposing the Clinton health care plan. The problem, though, was that members of the public, by their own admission, did not claim that their objections to Clinton's health care plan were based on a well-informed understanding of it. Only a small proportion of the electorate (about 20 percent) said they knew a lot about what was in Clinton's plan when it was announced, and that minority actually shrank as the congressional debate wore on.[59] By August 1994, the Harris poll was reporting that 13 percent of Americans felt well informed about the health care plan in general and 15 percent felt they had a good understanding of how the various reform proposals would affect them and their families.[60] In the midst of the health care debate in February 1994, most Americans did not grasp even the most basic features of the administration's plan. Only about one in four, for example, knew that Clinton was the principal sponsor of a health care bill that included an "employer mandate," under which employers had to provide health insurance to full-time employees.[61] At the close of 1995, a slightly larger proportion of the population—about a third—actually thought that Congress had already passed health care reform or didn't know whether legislation had been enacted.[62]

The press, which concentrated primarily on the legislative battle in Congress, may have exacerbated public ignorance by its narrow, garbled coverage of Clinton's plan. In one revealing experiment that was part of a larger study examining print coverage of health care reform, Professor Kathleen Jamieson and her colleague Joseph Cappella gave one group of adults 15 articles about health care reform to read, while a second group received one article on that topic and 14 articles on another subject. The group that had read 15 articles on health care reform knew no more about what was in the health care legislation than the group that read one article. Equally troubling, almost 75 percent of the adults polled in the professors' multicity survey said that the quality of their own health care would decrease or remain the same if news stories about the health proposals could be believed.[63]

In the end, the public's vague understanding of Clinton's health care proposal was that it would do little to help people who already had health insurance. Polls showed that voters wanted the costs of their own health care reined in, but the typical American didn't care deeply about providing coverage for the uninsured—particularly if doing so might conceivably raise costs, expand government intervention, or limit their own choice of medical care.

In Blendon's view, and that of other experts who tracked the voters' response to Clinton's initiative, the health care plan died because it failed the me-first test. In a 1995 article reviewing some 28 surveys on the health care debate, Blendon and his Harvard colleagues write that the polls disclosed that "from the outset Americans showed more concern for solving their own health care problems than those facing the nation as a whole. . . . Americans' strong support for reform could be quickly tempered by messages implying that personal sacrifices might be required to deal with broader problems."[64]

The public's insistence that reform " 'do no harm' to them personally," says Blendon, suggests that in the future, social policy initiatives that personally affect the majority of Americans will shrink to the least offensive common denominator. Not all social policies immediately affect most Americans at a personal level. Welfare reform does not. But major health care reforms and rewrites of the tax code do.

Already, the pattern that bedeviled Clinton's health care plan has undermined Republican efforts to reduce the growth of Medicare. Like Clinton, Newt Gingrich and the Republicans started off with substantial public support for reforming Medicare. In October 1995, 58 percent of the public thought Medicare had serious problems and needed major reform.[65] But support for a Medicare overhaul has dissipated, even though few members of the public understood the Republicans' 1996 proposal. Blendon points out that popular opposition mushroomed after a plurality of Americans became convinced that they would personally be worse off, ending up with less choice under the Republican plan once they themselves became eligible for Medicare.[66]

The mile-wide, inch-deep support for sweeping domestic reforms could soon sap the bipartisan effort to keep the budget balanced, too. Most voters believe that balancing the budget should be a top national priority. Yet only one in three Americans think they would personally be better off once the budget is balanced. Roughly one in five say they would be worse off.[67] "The notion of 'reform,'" says Blendon, "sounds good to the voters—until they think it may actually touch their lives."[68]

The Roots of the Optimism Gap

We [have] developed an affluence that reached down into almost every level of the working population to an extent that would have made the Sun King blink. . . . [It] has given us a sense of immunity to ordinary dangers.

Tom Wolfe[1]

The gap between voters' personal and public expectations is a long-standing one. What is new is that the optimism gap has widened so in the last decade that Americans now hold great expectations only for their family, their friends, and themselves.

How did the I'm OK–They're Not division become so deep? Before the advent of television, Americans tended more to "globalize." They assumed, that is, that what they knew from personal experience might be roughly true for the nation at large. Contrary to the oft-used aphorism, familiarity bred respect, not contempt.

Even in the "rebellious" 1960s and into the early 1970s, most Americans trusted institutions like the federal government and the public schools. In a 1973 Gallup poll, 60 percent of respondents said their children were getting a better elementary and high school education than they themselves had received, and only 20 percent thought it was worse; by 1994, 51 percent of the public thought the schools were worse than in their day.[2] Pollster Daniel Yankelovich writes that "from the late 1960s to the mid-1970s . . . the typical American attitude could be paraphrased as 'I'm doing okay. Why shouldn't others get a break too?' Majority attitudes toward government and private sector programs to help minorities were positive."[3] The mood of the time could be summed up in the pop psychology book *I'm O.K., You're O.K.,* which hit the *New York Times* bestseller list in 1972.

The Television Transformation

There are several plausible explanations for why Americans' appraisals of "others" dimmed after the mid-1970s. One possible cause, which has still not received the attention it merits, is television. Television is particularly likely to be central to the shift in public attitudes because Americans' pessimism about the world outside their communities is based largely on secondhand information, which they now gather chiefly from TV. The impact of television can be deceptive. Even though it may be the most filtered and distorted news medium, Americans trust news coverage on TV more than newspapers, and they have felt that way since the early 1960s.[4] Seeing and hearing a TV news story give it a vividness that the written word lacks. Viewers tend to trust television more than newspapers because they think they can tell better if someone is lying or concealing something if they can watch that person on camera. This exaggerated sense of intimacy and "reality" makes things seem worse than they are elsewhere in the nation, while diluting the impact of local nontelevised stories and word of mouth. "Any sense that things must be as they appear locally is . . . apt to be fatally undermined," as sociologist Craig Calhoun puts it.[5]

It is true that in the mid-1960s, before the optimism gap started to widen, the vast majority of American households already had televisions. Most viewers, however, didn't have the TV on nearly as long as they do today. On average, households with a TV now have at least one set on almost eight hours a day.[6] And a quarter century ago, the three networks, with their relatively bland fare, still dominated the market. As late as 1980, only 1 percent of households with television had VCRs, and just 20 percent had cable television.[7] By 1995, 81 percent of households with television had VCRs, and 63 percent were hooked up to cable.[8] The portrait of society that has emerged from popular Fox network shows such as *Married with Children* and *The Simpsons,* or cable offerings like *Beavis and Butt-head,* is far more fractious than what was provided by shows in the 1970s, like *The Mary Tyler Moore Show.*

Long-term regular exposure to television also appears to warp people's understanding of the world around them in ways that widen the optimism gap. Heavy television viewing makes "an independent contribution to the feeling of living in a mean and gloomy world," in the words of George Gerbner, the dean emeritus of the University of Pennsylvania's Annenberg School of Communication.[9] Numerous studies by Gerbner and his colleagues have shown that heavy viewers of television assume crime is rising even when it is falling. And moderate to heavy viewers, writes Gerbner, had a "higher level of general distrust of others and . . . felt that people, by and large, were just looking out for themselves."[10]

News coverage is not the only way TV has buttressed fear-

fulness and pessimism. Network prime-time programming became far more graphic in the last quarter century. For their 1994
book *Prime Time,* Robert Lichter, Linda Lichter, and Stanley
Rothman analyzed prime-time television series, randomly se-
lecting a total of 620 episodes that aired from 1955 to 1986. They
found that after 1975, the violent crime rate for television char-
acters was eight times as high as the violent crime rate citizens
actually reported in national victimization surveys. A typical
night of viewing (excluding news shows, movies, game shows,
and variety shows) included "about a dozen murders and fifteen
to twenty assorted robberies, rape, assaults, and other acts of
mayhem. . . . in real life, according to the FBI, violent crimes
account for about 5 percent of all arrests. On television they
make up 56 percent of all illegal acts."[11] The authors found
much the same pattern of decline conveyed in television's depic-
tion of sex. Before 1970, says Robert Lichter, television sex was
chiefly for people who were in love; after 1970, recreational sex
grew to the extent that, by the 1990s, TV depictions of it had
increased twentyfold.[12]

Despite its drawbacks, television can have a positive impact
on public attitudes. If used responsibly, television can foster
learning, and public television series like *Sesame Street* and *Mis-
ter Rogers' Neighborhood* have even been shown to boost children's vocabulary and grades.[13] Nor does television always make
viewers more distrustful or indifferent to the plight of others.
BBC news footage of horribly emaciated children in Ethiopia in
1984 created an outpouring of aid from Americans and made
the famine there real in ways that print reports failed to do.
When Princess Diana died in a car crash in 1997, the televised
coverage of her funeral prompted a worldwide outpouring of
grief that, momentarily at least, seemed to shrink people's sense
of distance from others. But these examples of television closing
social distance stand out partly because they seem like exceptions to the rule of how TV typically affects people.

The Expectations Explosion

Ironically, while TV was helping to lower Americans' assessment of other people's communities, it helped elevate viewers' expectations about personal prosperity and the defining characteristics of the "good life"—what it meant to be "OK." *Dallas* replaced *Peyton Place*; *Lifestyles of the Rich and Famous* replaced *Queen for a Day.* Televised materialism has become far more rampant. Today, children see roughly 20,000 commercials on the boob tube a year.[14]

With little notice, the nature of advertising has shifted in ways that seem to subtly reinforce people's sense of separateness from "others." For example, in his book *Breaking Up America,* Joseph Turow makes the case that ad agencies and media firms started about 15 years ago to make unprecedented attempts "to search out and exploit differences between consumers."[15] Anyone who has been bombarded with specialized mail-order catalogs is familiar with the enormous upsurge in targeted marketing in just a decade, along with the consumer cocoon it can create. The spread of cable television with its various signature shows has further fragmented and personalized the ad market. "If you are told over and over [in ads] that different kinds of people are not part of your world, you will be less and less likely to want to deal with those people," Turow argues.[16]

It is hard to prove or disprove whether Turow is right about the impact of modern-day advertising and direct mail. It is clear, though, that the dicing and slicing of America that he refers to is a pattern that has been repeated across much of the culture for the last quarter century. As columnist Robert Samuelson writes in *The Good Life and Its Discontents*:

> In the 1950s and early 1960s, everything seemed to foster greater national cohesion. New technologies (TV, jet travel, interstate

highways) shrank social distance and favored "mass" markets. Almost all adults shared the experiences of the Depression and the Second World War. Politics widened the "mainstream" to include those—notably, blacks and the poor—who had been most removed. But since then, everything has seemed to emphasize our differences. Income inequality has increased. Group consciousness (whether by women, blacks, ethnic groups, gay people, the disabled, or different generations) has risen. . . . Mass culture is receding before niche culture.[17]

As Samuelson points out in his book, the parents of the baby boomers who came of age during the depression and World War II had a much more modest sense of entitlement. They considered monotonous jobs, strained marriages, serious illnesses, economic recessions, and financial sacrifice to be part of the ordinary run of life. When they had children in the late 1940s, 1950s, and early 1960s, they were delighted and somewhat surprised by their own rapid rise in living standards. But their children had grander expectations of government to which politicians pandered. By 1965, Lyndon Johnson had proclaimed that the federal government could end poverty and eliminate recessions,[18] but it is hard to imagine Franklin Roosevelt or Dwight Eisenhower making similarly ambitious pronouncements.

Even though American workers continue to enjoy a rise in living standards—the after-tax income of Americans rose a hearty 58 percent on a per capita basis from 1970 to 1996, adjusted for inflation[19]—the baby boomers, unlike their parents, came of age at a time when rapid progress was considered a birthright rather than a blessing. And it wasn't just material progress that was preordained. Polls show that after the 1960s, members of the public felt jobs, marriages, and relationships had to be fulfilling. In 1962 the Gallup poll asked people what ingredients went into the "formula of success in today's

America"; only 6 percent of Americans cited having a job one enjoys. When Gallup asked much the same question in 1983, its pollsters found that having a job one enjoys (cited by 49 percent) was one of the top trappings of personal success.[20]

As the disposable income of Americans rose, consumers rediscovered French sociologist Emile Durkheim's pithy maxim, "The more one has the more one wants."[21] Baby boomers who now earn less than $30,000 a year say they would need $60,000 a year to fulfill all their dreams. Boomers making more than $100,000 a year say they would need a yearly income of $200,000.[22] Everyone seems to dream of having twice what they now have, no matter how much that is. Possessions and opportunities that most families deemed luxuries in the 1950s—such as attending college, or owning an air conditioner, dishwasher, or second car—have become virtual necessities in many households. So have items like a microwave oven and a VCR that did not even exist a generation ago. Since 1975, Roper Starch Worldwide has quizzed Americans on which of two dozen items they thought of when they imagined "the good life, the life you'd like to have." In the mid-1970s, most adults had modest aspirations: owning a home, a happy marriage, children who had the opportunity for a college education, a car, an interesting job, and a lawn.

Twenty years later, a majority of Americans think the good life includes a job that pays above average, a color TV, a college education for oneself, and having "a lot of money." Nearly half say that having a vacation home and a second car are an essential part of the good life.[23] When they were teenagers, most Americans would have deemed a family that owned a swimming pool to be of well-above-average wealth. Only 13 percent of adults would say the same today.[24]

Members of the public are well aware of this expectations explosion. In fact, they believe it is the prime reason that Americans in general feel so strapped today, even if they themselves don't. Less than a quarter of Americans believe that their parents' standard of living at its peak exceeded their own, or that their own standard of living has declined in the past 15 years. But that doesn't stop people from believing that the middle class as a whole is in dire financial straits.[25]

When the Roper Center for Public Opinion Research asked adults in 1996, "Generally speaking, do you feel the middle class in America is currently facing more economic hardship than at any other time during the past 50 years?" more than half of the respondents (55 percent) said there was more hardship now. Just 14 percent said there was less economic hardship today (with most of the rest saying the situation hadn't changed).[26] When asked, however, about the *cause* of these middle-class financial worries, the vast majority of Americans (63 percent) attributed them to "high expectations," not to genuine financial plight.[27]

In the end, it is the simultaneous inflation of personal expectations and the deflation of people's sense of the nation that Americans perceive as a painful mismatch. Consumers are currently chasing grander dreams in an ever-more-troubled world that seems less and less receptive to them. Political scientist James Q. Wilson perhaps best sums up the post-1970s expectation mismatch by observing: "Today, most of us have not merely the hope but enjoy the reality of a degree of comfort, freedom, and peace unparalleled in human history. And we can't stop complaining about it."[28]

Skewing the Market

People's innate tendency to think well of themselves explains why the I'm OK–They're Not syndrome has always troubled libertarians, and why, in recent years, it has started to concern some traditional Democrats and Republicans as well. Two centuries ago in *The Wealth of Nations*, Adam Smith recognized that the "invisible hand" of the market could be led awry by overconfident consumers. "The chance of gain is by every man more or less over-valued," he warned, "and the chance of loss is by most men under-valued."[29]

In countless daily decisions, the I'm OK–They're Not syndrome can painfully skew the workings of the free market. Virtually everyone has encountered naive college students who imagine that upon graduating, employers will welcome them and place them in a position of authority over other workers. But in their recent book *The-Winner-Take-All Society,* Robert H. Frank and Phillip J. Cook fret that this propensity of college graduates to exaggerate their talents is taking a more insidious turn. They suggest that students' inflated opinions of their employability is propelling them into overcrowded fields with a few visible rich superstars, while deterring them from pursuing careers in teaching, science, and government that provide more lasting social benefit. Many graduates of top schools fail to assess the job market accurately because they think they can emulate the success of a Michael Jordan, a Michael Eisner, or a Johnnie Cochran. Ultimately, Frank and Cook argue, those overconfident graduates exacerbate the nation's growing economic inequality by turning the job market into a place where only a relatively small number of winners make fabulous sums.[30]

Even sadder are the winner-takes-all pipe dreams of poor youngsters, especially black males who harbor unrealistic hopes of becoming professional athletes. The odds against a high school student going on to play professional sports are astronomical, about 10,000 to 1. Yet two in three black males ages 13 to 18 believe they can earn a living playing professional sports.[31] To take the most obvious downside of this phenomenon, *U.S. News & World Report* suggests in a recent cover story that black males' obsession with sports may be dissuading them from pursuing more realistic routes to upward mobility—namely, education.[32]

The impact of the optimism gap on the financial markets

and business decision making is harder to document, though numerous studies suggest it permeates the corporate board-rooms of even flinty-eyed executives. Ask the typical CEO to candidly predict the company's future performance, and he will anticipate more growth for his firm than for his competitors. (His production manager will likely overpredict production, too.)[33]

Several years ago, a Harvard Business School study of financial analysts, corporate executives, and portfolio managers found that all three groups agreed the stock market is too preoccupied with quarterly earnings. However, most company executives felt their own company was not inhibited by short-term market pressures. Only other companies tended to limit long-term investments because of short-term pressures. It does not take much imagination to see how this self-flattering image could lead portfolio managers to underestimate their competition and overestimate their financial acumen and intuition.[34]

The optimism gap can create the same deceptive skewing of choices in less formal markets, too. Consider the case of child care. In her book *It Takes a Village,* Hillary Rodham Clinton points out that "paradoxically, while many parents say that finding affordable child care is a major worry, the vast majority claim to be happy with their arrangements."[35] Clinton's comments refer to a massive national study published in 1995, which found that parents vastly exaggerate the quality of care their children receive. A third of parents with children in infant/toddler rooms had their babies in care that trained observers rated as poor. Yet not one of those parents gave the infant/toddler room a poor rating, and almost 90 percent felt their center was providing high-quality care.[36]

A final evaluation report by researchers at the University of Colorado at Denver concludes somberly "that there is no incentive for [child care] centers to produce higher levels of quality, and there may be a real [cost] disincentive to do[ing] so."[37] "Par-

ents often assume that cost is the biggest barrier to good care,"
Clinton concludes. "But another problem may be their inability
to recognize good quality and demand it for their children."[38]

Masters of Denial: Someone Else's Disease

Regardless of its causes, the optimism gap can have life-
threatening consequences. People at risk for AIDS, unintended
pregnancies, alcoholism, and smoking often fail to heed the
warnings of public health campaigns because "it won't happen
to me." "When it came to denial, I was an expert," writes bas-
ketball star Earvin "Magic" Johnson in his autobiography. "The
information I needed to protect myself [from contracting the
HIV virus] had been all around me. It was right there in my
face—on radio and TV, in newspapers and magazines, in locker
room lectures. But I didn't pay attention. I didn't think it could
happen to me."[39] Johnson's thinking, as he later summarized,
was that "AIDS was someone else's disease. It was a disease for
gays and drug users."[40]

Magic Johnson's assumption that AIDS "couldn't happen
to me" is, in fact, the way many Americans think about the
worst public health scourges of modern society. "I honestly believed I had a better chance of winning the lottery than contracting this disease," boxer Tommy Morrison confessed after he,
too, tested HIV positive. "I thought I was bulletproof."[41] Morrison is not alone. Stand 100 Americans in a room and ask them
to sit, one by one, if they have driven a car without buckling a
seat belt, jaywalked in busy traffic, smoked a cigarette, or engaged in other known risky behavior, and before long, everyone
in the room is sitting.

Studies have shown repeatedly that whether the problem is
unintended pregnancy, addiction to cigarettes, liquor, and
drugs, or contracting AIDS, members of the public assume both
that other people are more likely to be afflicted by such ills and

that if they themselves are afflicted, they will be able to handle their addiction or illness without suffering the life-threatening consequences that plague others.[42] Most people at risk have a George Burns story to comfort them: The relative who just hit 100 years old and still smokes cigars every day, the elderly aunt who downs a tumbler of whiskey each morning, and so on.

This I-am-a-rock conviction thwarts policymakers who seek to mount public health campaigns to reduce alcohol and drug abuse, teen pregnancy, sexually transmitted diseases, AIDS, and other behaviorally related illnesses. Without surefire cures, government officials have no choice but to rely heavily on public service announcements, educational campaigns, and preventive measures to reduce risky behavior. But due to the I'm OK–They're Not syndrome, many intended targets of public health campaigns also assume—just as Magic Johnson did—that the government's warnings are intended for "someone else."

The history of AIDS prevention efforts is illustrative. After several years of initial confusion and misinformation in the 1980s, Americans of all stripes now know how the HIV virus is and is not transmitted. The problem confronting public health officials today is no longer ignorance but rather denial and fatalism. David McKirnan, a psychologist at the University of Illinois at Chicago who counsels individuals still engaged in high-risk behaviors, says that "you can't find a gay man any more who does not know how HIV is transmitted. And yet study after study shows very high continuance of high-risk behaviors, especially among young gay men and minorities."[43]

A rare 1990–91 national survey that sampled heavily in high-risk urban areas found that just 37 percent of those with one or more risk factors for AIDS had been tested for HIV antibody. Condom use among those at risk for HIV was disappointingly low, too. Only 17 percent of those with multiple sex partners, 13 percent of those with risky sex partners, and 11 percent of individuals who had received blood in earlier years (but not been tested for HIV) used condoms all the time.[44]

The power of denial, and the toll of the optimism gap, are painfully evident at the sexually transmitted disease (STD) department at Miami's main public health clinic, which has one of the highest HIV rates in the United States. In 1989–90, 12 percent of its clients were HIV positive.[45] Beginning in December 1987, the clinic started providing counseling about HIV and offered HIV testing to all its patients. It also offered posttest educational sessions about reducing risk. Yet during the next two years, clinic officials discovered that clients who tested HIV negative actually *increased* their high-risk behavior. Of HIV-negative patients who returned on their own for test results, the percentage with gonorrhea or a new STD increased 106 percent and 103 percent, respectively, after posttest counseling.[46]

Terry Tucker, who formerly oversaw the clinic, says that "once a client has had a negative test it's hard to convince them that they may not continue to dodge the bullet."[47] Denial at the clinic comes in many shapes and forms. Some of the young men who had spent time in the penal system and had periodically engaged in homosexual acts insist they are not at risk and are not "gay" because they were the one who penetrated their partners. Bisexual males also don't identify themselves as gay, and they claim they are not at risk for AIDS either. Others cite testing negative to HIV as proof they are invulnerable to AIDS.

"The condom broke" or "she looked clean" are routine excuses for positive blood tests. Bruce Heath, who has counseled hundreds of patients in his years at the clinic, says that "a lot of Cuban men, black men, and white men will say, 'I'm not at risk because I'm not having sex with men or injecting drugs.' Then I'll ask them how many partners they've had in the last year, and they'll say, 'Oh, I've slept with 15 prostitutes—but I'm not at risk.' "[48]

Denial, though, is not reserved for the disadvantaged and

uneducated. Ask Kirk Arthur, who had lived in six countries and spoke three languages fluently by the time he was 15. When he moved with his affluent family to Safety Harbor, Florida, as a teenager in the mid-1980s, it simply didn't occur to him that he could get HIV. Safety Harbor then was everything its name implied: a politically conservative town on Old Tampa Bay on the Gulf coast, where people often left their doors unlocked at night. Outside Arthur's window was a large pasture.

One night at the age of 19, Arthur set out to lose his virginity with another man. Drunk on beer, he got picked up and had unprotected sex. Afterward, he wondered whether he should have used a condom but thought, "Hey, this is Safety Harbor." When, two relationships later, at the age of 21, Arthur went into the public health department for an HIV test, the nurse told him much the same thing. Arthur explained to the nurse, an acquaintance of his, that he had had one unprotected sexual encounter at 19 but had used condoms since then. "Don't worry," she told him, "we've never had a case of AIDS here. This obviously is not your problem."

The nurse was wrong. When Arthur learned he was HIV positive, he called his mother at work and the two walked around a mall for hours, alternately crying, wondering what to do next, and observing, in Arthur's words, "how suddenly silly the mannequins looked." Seven years later, Arthur is still asymptomatic but is bereft of his illusions of invulnerability. "It's very easy," he cautions, "to think that education and affluence are insulation against something as horrible as AIDS."[49]

The Self-Admiring American

The overweening conceit which the greater part of men have of their own abilities is an ancient evil remarked by the philosophers and moralists of all ages. Their absurd presumption in their own good fortune has been less taken notice of. It is, however, if possible, still more universal. There is no man living who, when in tolerable health and spirits, has not some share of it.

ADAM SMITH[1]

In the spring of 1997, *U.S. News & World Report* commissioned a survey that asked Americans to handicap the odds that 15 assorted celebrities would get into heaven. Not surprisingly, Americans felt that O. J. Simpson, Dennis Rodman, and radio shock-jock Howard Stern had little chance of passing muster with Saint Peter. Topping the list of famous people headed for heaven was Mother Teresa; nearly 80 percent of Americans thought it likely that the Nobel peace prize winner would get her wings. But here was the survey's most startling finding: The individual that Americans thought most likely to enter the pearly gates was—well, themselves. Eighty-seven percent of Americans thought that they were heaven-bound, compared to 79 percent who thought the same of Mother Teresa.[2] At the time of the *U.S. News* poll, Mother Teresa had not yet died. But according to the Gallup poll's annual year-end survey, she was then Americans' choice for the most admired woman in the world.[3]

The fact that the average American thinks he or she is more likely to go to heaven than Mother Teresa provides an amusing if telltale glimpse at how Americans see themselves and the world around them. A *Wall Street Journal* poll taken shortly before the *U.S. News* survey suggests that Americans think they are bound for the afterlife because they hold an extremely generous opinion of their own morals. The *Journal* wryly noted that "if you can believe them, most Americans are closer to canonization than damnation, even though they say in general, Americans' morals are poor and getting worse. When asked to rate their own morals and values on a scale of one to 100, with one being totally depraved and 100 being pure as the driven snow, exactly half gave themselves a score of 90 or above. Only 11% rated their morals below 75."[4]

It is not wholly unexpected that Americans have an exalted impression of their own virtues. Over the centuries, many thinkers have commented on people's proclivity to think well of themselves. "Man prefers to believe what he prefers to be true," as the English philosopher Francis Bacon put it.[5] Only in this century, though, have researchers begun to systematically document the scope of the I'm OK–They're Not syndrome. Social psychologists have labeled the optimism gap and its offshoots with such terms as "self-serving bias," "unrealistic optimism," and "optimistic bias."

Initially, those most interested in researching the optimism gap were social psychologists. In more recent decades, political scientists and pollsters have expanded on their work, though the two communities of analysts have done little to link their respective findings. When the evidence is added up, however, it shows that the I'm OK–They're Not syndrome pervades the thinking of Americans to an astonishing degree.

The earliest studies by psychologists tracked what college students thought of their own intelligence and scholastic abilities. They discovered that hardly any students considered themselves to be less intelligent than their peers. A survey of freshmen at the University of Wyoming in the 1920s found that 71 percent thought they were smarter than their fellow students.[6] In 1949, administrators at Kansas State decided to ask freshmen a battery of questions about their self-perceived scholastic abilities, after college counselors became concerned about students who were rationalizing away their poor performance in school. Freshmen who were flunking out seemed to make less use of faculty advisers and recognized fewer academic problems than those who were succeeding. It turned out, though, that few of the freshmen were worried about whether they had the right stuff. Sixty-two percent predicted they would test in the top quarter of their class, and more than 90 percent anticipated they would test in the upper half of their class.[7]

By the early 1960s, the concern of the educational establishment had shifted. Sociologists wanted to find out what adults thought about the sweeping use of standardized intelligence tests. As a result of this newfound interest, the Russell Sage Foundation sponsored a survey of some 1,500 U.S. adults in 1963 that asked people to judge how intelligent they were compared to other individuals and family members. Once again, less than 10 percent of those surveyed thought they were less intelligent than nonfamily members. Quoting the inimitable wisdom of cartoon character Yogi Bear's theme song, the researchers concluded that most people ultimately believe they are "smarter than the average bear."[8]

One might guess that well-educated university professors would be less susceptible to self-serving bias, since they could anticipate that half of them had to be below average when compared to their peers. Yet the vast majority of college faculty—94 percent in a mid-1970s survey at the University of Nebraska,[9] 90 percent in a 1977–78 survey of college faculty at 24 other institutions[10]—rated themselves as superior to their average colleague, too. "Faculty relegate to myth the idea that there is an epidemic of poor teaching in higher education," a team of researchers concluded. "Although faculty committees may vote for instructional improvement programs, it is not . . . because *they* need one, but because they believe *their colleagues* do."[11]

By the end of the 1970s, it was clear that not only did college students still have a high opinion of their talents, but they also felt the rest of the world was in pretty sorry shape. Large-scale surveys by the Carnegie Foundation found that while more than 90 percent of students were optimistic about their own future, only 41 percent felt the same way about the nation. The undergraduates, as a book at the time put it, believed they were "going first class on the Titanic."[12]

How does self-serving bias originate? Psychologists believe unrealistic optimism is an inevitable part of the human condition. As William James once wrote, "No fact in human nature is more characteristic than its willingness to live on a chance."[13] Even residents of a notoriously dangerous, run-down housing project display old-fashioned hometown pride, much like the inhabitants of Garrison Keillor's mythic Lake Wobegon, where all the women are strong, all the men are good-looking, and all the children are above average.

The View from a High-rise Graveyard

There are not many worse spots in America to live than Chicago's Cabrini-Green housing projects. In the early 1980s, former Chicago mayor Jane Byrne moved into the high-rise developments for several weeks to dramatize the dilapidated living conditions, drug dealing, and local gang problems.[14] In 1992, Cabrini-Green achieved international notoriety when Dantrell Davis, a seven-year-old, was gunned down by a sniper in a project courtyard on his way to school, as he held his mother's hand.[15] Five years later, Cabrini-Green was back in the news after a nine-year-old girl identified only as "Girl X" was raped, choked, poisoned, and dumped in a stairwell, with gang markings scrawled across her body.[16] Vincent Lane, who was chairman of the Chicago Housing Authority (CHA) from 1988 until May 1995 (when the federal government took over the beleaguered agency), calls Cabrini-Green the symbol of "all that's bad in public housing."[17] News accounts over the years have even likened the tenements to a "high-rise graveyard" or, more pointedly, "hell on earth."[18]

Relatively few news stories, however, have underscored some startling realities that first surfaced in a 1986 tenant survey of three infamous Chicago high-rise buildings, one of them in Cabrini-Green. Roughly four in five residents in the Cabrini-Green tenement turned out to *like* their apartments, and nearly half (41 percent) preferred a high-rise development to other living options. In fact, Cabrini-Green tenants didn't seem desperate to leave; on average, they had lived in their current apartments for 8 years and in CHA housing for 16 years.[19]

Today, longtime tenants acknowledge that the development has serious gang and drug problems. Perhaps half of the residents are looking to move. Yet a surprising number of tenants reject the notion that the project's problems are all that different from those of other Chicago neighborhoods. Joyce Flake, who moved to Cabrini-Green in 1985 and now works as a security guard there, says that "I think Cabrini-Green is one of the safest places to live. None of my children have ever been hurt or attacked, and everyone knows us here. You know drugs are everywhere in Chicago. Pilots are using drugs; you can't find a drug-free workplace in the city, even at city hall."[20]

Willie Bell Harris has lived at Cabrini-Green since 1964, even though her husband was murdered in the development in 1974 when, she recalls, he was mistaken for someone else with a similar jacket. "I stayed on in Cabrini-Green because it's the safest place to live," Harris insists. "I've never been attacked once. My apartment is large, safe, and cheap, and I don't have to worry about it burning down. It's no different here than anywhere else. The gangs and drugs are just less visible in the suburbs."[21]

Much like tenants in other cities who seek to live in public housing projects, Flake, Harris, and other residents cite numerous virtues to their high-rise apartments. They like not having to cut the lawn and shovel the snow, and enjoy the sweeping views of Chicago's downtown Loop from the upper floors of the developments. They also appreciate the easy walking access to health clinics, swimming pools, parks, and a nearby upscale shopping district. Both Flake and Harris refer to the sense of "family" they share with neighbors, who hold joint barbecues, pick up diapers for each other, pitch in to help out if someone is a few dollars short on the rent, and walk other people's children to school. When Harris had her first heart attack in 1989, neighbors on her floor's informal "sick committee" took care of two of her grandchildren for two weeks.

For several years, ex–CHA chairman Lane sought to redevelop several of the Cabrini-Green tenements as mixed-income duplexes and town houses. Trying to empty some buildings, the

CHA offered residents a housing voucher they could use to rent a private apartment, an apartment in another CHA development, CHA scattered site housing, or the right to stay put until replacement housing was built. For those willing to move, CHA offered to hire and pay a professional moving company, provide boxes to pack belongings, and disconnect and reconnect tenants' phones and cable television. The agency also took residents on bus tours so they could visit other scattered housing sites and housing voucher units to see what they looked like.

Despite the CHA relocation assistance, only about half of the residents wanted to move. For more than two years, Joyce Flake fought CHA plans to demolish her high-rise. She even took part in demonstrations held by Cabrini tenants outside the mayor's office and CHA headquarters to protest the agency's relocation plans. With only about 25 families left in her huge high-rise, Flake finally gave in and moved to an apartment a block away in November 1996.[22] She explained her reluctance to move by saying, "If I move, I have to meet new people, and my 15-year-old son might get hurt because he is a new face. I'm afraid to move out of this neighborhood."

While it may not be immediately evident, the controversy at Cabrini-Green is in some ways a microcosm of the nation's long-running debate about how to best respond to ghetto poverty. Since at least the 1960s, politicians, urban planners, and scholars have split over whether government policies should encourage ghetto residents to stay in their neighborhood and redevelop it or to move up and out to better areas.

In the 1960s, liberals tended to favor the community redevelopment strategies. They promoted enterprise zones to provide tax breaks to businesses willing to remain in poor neighborhoods and sought to bolster community action groups through the War on Poverty. Conservatives initially derided such programs as building the "gilded ghetto." Today, however, it is conservatives who usually promote enterprise zones, tenant ownership of public housing, and various community "self-help" strategies for the inner city. Many liberals, meanwhile, have shifted sides, too. They now favor "mobility programs," such as vans that carpool inner-city workers out to suburban job sites, and the much-lauded Gautreaux program, which has subsidized low-income black families in Chicago's public housing who are looking to move into private-market housing and nearby suburbs.

The attachment of Cabrini-Green tenants to their homes, and their skeptical response to the housing authority's relocation efforts, are not unusual. Surveys of other housing projects in Chicago, and of inner-city neighborhoods elsewhere in the nation, have also shown that many residents are reasonably content and have created community ties.[23] Vincent Lane explains the opposition of the Cabrini-Green residents to relocating by saying, "It was the devil they knew versus the devil they don't know." Lane points out that the besieged tenants' fear of change is hardly unique. "Why," he asks, "do people stay in northern Ireland despite the shooting and violence over the years?"[24]

Hope Springs Internal: The Causes of Unrealistic Optimism

Most Americans fall prey to the I'm OK–They're Not syndrome. Rich, poor, black, white, well educated, ill educated, young, old—virtually all groups of Americans simultaneously hold sanguine views of themselves and pessimistic appraisals of others.[25] Yet the optimism gap is not just a private abstraction that people carry around inside their heads. As the preceding case studies have illustrated, the I'm OK–They're Not syndrome is woven into the daily lives of Americans.

Why is the syndrome so powerful? Anthropologist Lionel Tiger argues that optimistically calculating one's odds "is as basic a human action as seeking food when hungry or craving fresh air in a dump."[26] Just as Cabrini-Green residents value the size and location of their apartments, so, too, most Americans selectively prize the more favorable aspects of their own lives. In explaining why people believe they are better-than-average drivers, for example, the economist Thomas Schelling points out that "everybody ranks himself high in qualities he values: careful drivers give weight to care, skillful drivers give weight to skill, and those who think that, whatever else they are not, at least they are polite, give weight to courtesy, and come out high on their own scale. This is the way that every child has the best dog on the block."[27]

In the abstract, the motives behind people's unrealistic optimism seem embarrassingly transparent. Of course, most people prefer to feel smarter and better than others! Feeling safe, in control, and invulnerable is better than feeling anxious or inferior. In practice, however, an individual's lofty opinion of himself or herself often seems quite rational and factual.

The pervasiveness of the optimism gap does not necessarily demonstrate that the public is self-deluded. At the very least, for example, half the electorate could correctly assume that they *do* fare better than the "average" citizen—and who can accurately guess where that dividing line falls, anyway?

The truth is that it is difficult to spot unrealistic optimism in yourself. People are always more familiar with their own attempts to act responsibly and solve problems than with the parallel efforts of others. A woman may plausibly think that she is less at risk than the average woman for, say, an unintended pregnancy because she knows more about her own capacity to use contraception or abstain from sex than she knows about a stranger's ability to do so.

At the same time, people rarely hear unvarnished opinions from the outside world about their shortcomings. Most strangers, and even friends, hedge their negative opinions of others when dealing with them face-to-face. If an incompetent employee turns in a subpar report, his or her boss is more likely to say "This needs some work" than "Now I know you are an idiot." This verbal trimming of the sails, repeated over and over again, can mislead people into thinking they are doing fine when they are coming up short.

One might similarly conclude that unrealistic optimism is really an artifact of survey methodology. That is, people are naturally reluctant to volunteer unflattering information about themselves and their families to a stranger or outsider. In fact, the optimism gap is much more than just a methodological quirk. Americans' optimistic bias about themselves shows up repeatedly, whether researchers use anonymous surveys, perform face-to-face interviews, or provide respondents with information first that should temper their personal optimism. As David Myers summarizes in his textbook *Social Psychology,* "The fact that the bias is as strong (or more strongly) evident when people respond privately suggests that people do genuinely *perceive* themselves in self-enhancing ways."[28]

Today, decades after the first surveys of college students took place, social psychologists have compiled a huge if little-appreciated literature on unrealistic optimism.[29] "One of the most documented findings in psychology," writes Thomas Gilovich, "is that the average person purports to believe extremely flattering things about him- or herself."[30] Unlike many syndromes, self-serving bias seems to be unaffected by age, sex, race, education, or occupation. In *Positive Illusions,* Shelley Taylor provides a sense of how omnipresent unrealistic optimism is among college students and older adults:

> Students asked to envision what their future lives would be like said they were more likely to graduate at the top of the class, get a good job, have a high starting salary, like their first job, receive an award for work, get written up in the paper, and give birth

to a gifted child than their classmates. Moreover, they considered themselves far less likely than their classmates to have a drinking problem, to be fired from a job, to get divorced after a few years of marriage, to become depressed, or to have a heart attack or contract cancer. . . . Older adults also underestimate the likelihood that they will encounter a large number of negative, but unhappily common, events such as having . . . job problems, contracting major diseases, or becoming depressed.[31]

Americans' conviction that they face fewer health risks than their peers has an equally broad scope. Several years ago, Professor Neil Weinstein, a leading researcher on unrealistic optimism, surveyed residents of New Brunswick, New Jersey, about the comparative health risks they faced. He asked them whether, when compared to men and women of their age, their risk was average, below average, or above average for 32 hazards. In all but one case (in this instance, contracting cancer), people thought their risk was below average.

People believed they were less at risk than others for drug addiction, poison ivy, sunstroke, a nervous breakdown, attempting suicide, becoming a homicide or mugging victim, having a serious auto injury, becoming senile, and getting gum disease or tooth decay.[32] Other studies have shown that people even assume that chemicals in food are more likely to afflict other people than themselves. Most Americans think they are less at risk than other people for being harmed by artificial sweeteners, caffeine, food additives, bacterial contamination of food, alcohol, or food irradiation.[33]

One thread connecting people's attitudes toward these various risks is that most individuals infer that hazards or tragedies can be avoided or minimized by responsible individuals like themselves. Americans are much less likely to think they have a unique invulnerability to the ultimately unavoidable (e.g., the common cold) than they are to events that are controllable (e.g., developing tooth decay).[34] Often, members of the public reduce estimates of their own risk by drawing conclusions based on a small number of visible, stereotypical victims: Only repressed adults develop ulcers, only people who fail to take precautions get mugged, and so on. This exaggerated sense of personal savvy is also evident in Americans' propensity to say they are above average in terms of nebulously defined traits (like their ability as "a conversationalist") rather than quantifiable traits (like their math aptitude test scores).[35]

As a rule, people show more self-serving bias the closer they get to home. In descending order, Americans are most optimistic about themselves, then come family and friends, with average "others" or strangers bringing up the rear. For example, in the *U.S. News & World Report* poll about heaven, 55 percent of Americans said at least half of their friends would get into heaven; 43 percent said at least half of their neighbors would get in; and just 30 percent said at least half of average Americans would make it.[36]

Even those numbers, however, don't fully convey just how wide the optimism gap is on many social issues. One way to illustrate the gulf is to ask people to quantify the odds that a problem will afflict them, their friends, or strangers, and then average out their responses. In a survey taken several years ago at the University of New Haven, students estimated the odds that the average undergraduate would acquire HIV through sex at 1 in 10. They next placed their friends' odds at 1 in 33. For themselves, the students saw the odds at 1 in a 1,000.[37] It's not just naive undergrads who make those kinds of projections, either. Women in the Marine Corps, for example, are even more sanguine about their chances of avoiding AIDS. They estimated that the average woman marine had a 1 in 429 chance of getting HIV or AIDS during the upcoming year, while their peers had a 1 in 1,535 chance. They figured their own odds of contracting the virus during the next year at 1 in 19,815.[38] As the Welsh social reformer Robert Owen summed up over a century ago upon separating from his business partner, "All the world is queer save thee and me, and even thou art a little queer."[39]

The Worldview

Most voters and public officials tend to be acquainted with the I'm OK–They're Not syndrome in a piecemeal fashion. Perhaps they have heard that taxpayers believe their own congressional representative does a good job but Congress does a lousy job. Or that people like the local public school but think that public schools in general are a mess. Yet those illustrations of the optimism gap are not isolated examples. As the psychological studies of optimistic bias suggest, and as polling data in recent decades confirm, the I'm OK–They're Not syndrome is a way of being, a kind of lens through which Americans now filter the world.

On issue after issue, Americans are repeatedly dividing the world into two camps. In the first camp, the one that is flourishing, they place themselves, their family, and their best friends. Everyone else belongs in the second camp, the one that is filled with sadsacks, is short on supplies, and is on the verge of mutiny.

Unlike the social psychologists, who studied unrealistic optimism to learn more about its link to human motivation, political scientists and pollsters have dissected the same phenomena for clues about electoral outcomes and public trust of government. The first such study was done in 1973 by the Institute for Social Research at the University of Michigan, which surveyed roughly 1,400 adults to see how they felt about the treatment they had received from agency staff in field offices of welfare, Medicare and Medicaid, state employment, and workers' compensation.

Contrary to the bureaucrat-hating stereotype, members of

the public were actually quite pleased with the way government offices responded to their problems. More than 70 percent said they were satisfied with the service they had gotten, felt that government employees had treated them fairly and considerately, and believed the agency had resolved their problems. Yet people's generally positive personal experience with various government offices did not translate into a good opinion of government offices per se. Only a little more than 30 percent of those surveyed thought government offices in general provided considerate treatment or did a good job of taking care of problems.[40]

The public's wan faith in government was particularly worrisome because, on the one hand, people's positive personal experiences failed to boost their opinion of most government agencies, and on the other, negative personal experiences increased their distrust of government. "It is almost as if agency people can do nothing to improve the general public image of government offices through consideration of clients and fairness of treatment, but they can do a great deal to impair it by unfair and inconsiderate handling of clients," the researchers concluded. "Good experience is the equivalent of no experience."[41]

Political scientists soon found a similar disconnect between personal experience and public belief while studying the comparative lack of class consciousness in the United States. Why did the cry "workers of the world unite" ring hollow in this nation, and why had socialism failed to catch on in America as it had in other Western democracies? One reason, documented in Kay Lehman Schlozman and Sidney Verba's 1979 book *Injury to Insult,* was that even unemployed workers—the so-called lumpenproletariat—did not become disenchanted with the American system or the opportunities available to them and their children. The jobless seemed to have an "invisible barrier between personal experience and abstract ideology," as the authors put it.[42]

Pollsters and political scientists discovered the same divide between personal experience and beliefs about society when they started analyzing people's voting patterns. For decades, politicians and pollsters have known that the condition of the economy plays an important role in how people vote. At first, the conventional wisdom was that people simply voted their pocketbooks. If they personally were doing well, they voted for the incumbent; if they were faring poorly, they voted for the challenger.

Starting sometime in the 1970s, however, it became clear that people often did *not* vote their pocketbooks. In the early 1980s, for example, Iowa farmers suffered a wave of foreclosures and their most dire period of economic distress in decades. Ronald Reagan was president during the farm crisis. If farmers were prepared to vote their pocketbooks, Walter Mondale should have gotten the vote of Iowa farmers in 1984. He didn't. The reason, surveys at the time showed, was that the farmers had more faith that Reagan would be able to turn around the economy in the future.[43]

From episodes such as these, political scientists have developed the notion of "sociotropic" voting. This is a fancy way of saying that people cast their votes based less on their own financial success than on how they think the nation is faring economically, or how they believe a candidate will influence the overall course of the economy in the years ahead.

In the last 15 years, as politicians' use of surveys has exploded, pollsters have broadened their research into why people vote as they do. Repeatedly, they have discovered the same "invisible barrier" between personal experience and public ideology that earlier political scientists documented. From issue to issue, Americans say they are far more optimistic about their own lives and their own communities than they are about other people's communities and the country at large.

In 1996, a Gallup poll asked some 2,000 Americans to pick from a list the one word that best described their feelings toward various institutions in the country. People could say they

Familiarity Breeds Respect

INSTITUTION/CONDITION	ENTHUSIASTIC, PLEASED, OR CONTENTED	WORRIED, AFRAID, OR UPSET
Condition of the American economy	20%	56%
Own community's economic situation	59	29
Personal financial situation	65	26
Country's moral and ethical condition	17	59
Community's moral and ethical condition	53	30
Personal spiritual condition	84	6
Condition of American families	25	60
Family life in local community	68	22
Your family	90	6
Nation's schools	29	54
Condition of the local schools	47	36
Elected officials in Washington	18	44
Local elected officials	55	22
Nation's churches	57	20
Condition of local churches	75	10
Your church or fellowship	74	4

SOURCE: Adapted from James Davison Hunter and Carl Bowman, *The State of Disunion: 1996 Survey of American Political Culture,* vol. 2, summary tables, the Post-Modernity Project, University of Virginia (In Medias Res Educational Foundation, Ivy, Va.), 1996.

felt enthusiastic, pleased, or contented; confused, worried, afraid, or upset; resentful or angry; or indifferent. The results showed that people's feelings differed dramatically depending on their locale. The table above illustrating the community/national gap is adapted from James Davison Hunter and Carl Bowman's *The State of Disunion* (which reported the results of the Gallup poll). The table shows, at the local, national, and personal level (where available), the proportion of Americans who were enthusiastic, pleased, or contented with various institutions versus the proportion who were worried, afraid, or upset.

As the table illustrates, the majority of Americans have diametrically opposed feelings about conditions in the country at large and conditions locally. Most people are worried, afraid, or upset about matters at the national level. Yet they are enthusiastic, pleased, or contented about those same issues at the local level. Even fewer members of the public personally fret about their finances, morals, and families. The only national institution that a majority of Americans still seem to have faith in are the country's churches (though churches are looked upon more favorably at the local level, too).

This split vision of the world extends well beyond the issues in the Gallup poll. It fosters a double image of most of the nation's leading social problems. Americans show the same polarized views on national and local conditions when they evaluate the state of race relations, pollution problems, drug abuse, violent crime, gang violence, school violence, child sex abuse, and crime prevention.[44]

At the personal level, Americans attest that they have little difficulty living up to their commitments to family and employers, they like their jobs and consider them secure, they are more religious today than in the past, they are blessed by caring, competent doctors who don't seek to rip them off. They are optimistic about what the future holds and are generally well on their way to fulfilling the American Dream. At the national level, though, Americans are convinced that people routinely fail to live up to their commitments, that job insecurity is rampant, that the importance of religion is receding, that doctors and hospitals are ripping off patients, that matters for the next generation are only going to get worse, and that it is impossible for most people anymore to fulfill the American Dream.

The gap between people's assessment of their private and

public worlds is wider than ever, as illustrated by a 1996 survey published in 1997 by the Pew Research Center, cited in the opening pages of the first chapter of this book. But the Pew survey also suggests that the optimism gap has changed in two other respects: It's now more partisan, and pessimism about America has grown mostly among young adults and baby boomers. A quarter century ago, Democrats and Republicans did not differ much when asked to rate the country's future. Today, Republicans are very pessimistic about the country's future, and Democrats are comparatively upbeat.[45] At the same time, adults of all ages once thought the state of the nation was better than they think it is now. Today, a generation gap has opened in people's assessments of the country, with only the elderly likely to give a high rating to the state of the nation.[46]

It's worth noting that the notion that the country is headed for hell in a handbasket is not just an inchoate sentiment, like the kvetching of Doug and Wendy Whiner in their memorable *Saturday Night Live* skits. The Pew study asked Americans about the status of 17 national problems. In 15 of the cases, majorities or pluralities said the country was losing ground. A majority of adults said that crime, drugs, moral standards, the public schools, job security, poverty, hunger and homelessness, the health care system, and Social Security and Medicare were all getting worse. A plurality thought the country was also losing ground on the deficit, illegal immigration, political corruption, the welfare system, and racial conflict. In only two areas—the environment and discrimination against minorities—did more Americans think the nation was making progress than thought it was regressing.[47]

American Exceptionalism

Is the I'm OK–They're Not syndrome uniquely American, or is it just as pronounced in other nations? In most industrialized nations, citizens do look more favorably on their own lives than on other people's lives and the state of the nation. As social psychologists have shown, the optimism gap is part and parcel of human nature. But while it originates in the human psyche, the optimism gap can widen or narrow depending on the times and tradition.

The 1995 Gallup poll referred to in the introduction suggests that the optimism gap is much wider in the United States than in other countries. Several causes may account for the differences. For starters, the United States is not currently in the midst of a national or international crisis. At moments of crisis, people are less likely to think of themselves as different from their neighbors. For example, many Americans now think of today's poor families as the "undeserving poor," families who are scamming the welfare system and refusing to work. Harvard professor David Ellwood, one of the chief architects of Bill Clinton's stillborn 1994 welfare reform proposal, lamented not long after he left the administration that "one of my greatest frustrations is that welfare has become so much about us versus them: 'What's wrong with these people?' "[48] Yet creating that kind of social distance from the poor was much harder, say, during the Great Depression. As sociologist Susan Mayer points out, the poor then "were no longer a morally corrupt fringe; they were one's neighbor, one's friend or oneself. The Great Depression demonstrated to many Americans that poverty was sometimes the result of bad luck rather than weak character."[49]

Unlike some developing countries, the United States has also had two other forces at work that have widened the optimism gap. First of all, it has well-developed media. In smaller nations, and in countries without such an extensive television and cable broadcast system, people are more likely than in the United States to rely on word of mouth, personal experience, oral traditions, and the like to form their judgments of other citizens.[50] Americans' reliance on television for news about other citizens and neighborhoods has left them dependent on a medium that displays both a potent and grim picture of other people's communities. In contrast to most nations—where people are today actually *more* likely to believe that people can be trusted than a couple of decades ago—Americans' distrust of the masses (i.e., their distrust of "most people") has grown since the 1960s.[51] Second, the United States experienced a period of prolonged and rapid economic progress followed by a period of slower progress after the 1950s and 1960s. Baby boomers would undoubtedly be less gloomy about today's robust economy if they had grown up during the depression, rather than in an era when housing costs were low and real wages doubled.

In short, while the I'm OK–They're Not syndrome reflects human nature, it can also be altered by history and culture. Several studies suggest that Chinese and Japanese students—reared by parents who encourage humility and self-effacement—do not display the self-serving bias that American students do. When researchers asked Japanese students what proportion of students in their university had higher intellectual abilities than themselves, had more athletic ability, or were more independent, the typical Japanese student estimated accurately that about 50 percent of his fellow students were smarter than he or she or had more of a given ability.[52]

Compared to parents of other nationalities, Americans often seem especially preoccupied with promoting their children's self-esteem. "Doonesbury" and other political cartoons have periodically mocked the self-esteem movement in schools. But it may have inflated the exalted image that many American students already had of themselves and thus inadvertently widened the optimism gap. If there is one thing that today's college students don't appear to suffer from, it is a lack of self-esteem. Since 1966, the Higher Education Research Institute at the University of California, Los Angeles, and the American Council of Education have sponsored massive, annual questionnaire surveys of college freshmen. In a typical year, more than 200,000 freshmen fill out the questionnaire. In 1996, a record proportion of freshmen ranked themselves above average (or in the top 10%) among people their age in terms of their academic ability (57.9%), leadership ability (53.6%), writing ability (41.7%), public speaking ability (30.1%), and artistic ability (26.1%).[53] Their self-ratings of intellectual self-confidence and social self-confidence were at near record highs, too. An extremely small proportion of freshmen (generally less than 10%) actually thought any of their abilities were below average.[54] On the whole, the surveys showed that college freshmen had a more inflated opinion of their brainpower and abilities in 1996 than in any of the previous 30 years.

The Benefits of "Unrealistic" Optimism

Those who struggle with depression or cynicism may think it odd to describe America as a nation overflowing with self-confident individuals. What about all the neurotic Americans, the Woody Allen types who think, as Groucho Marx put it, that "I don't want to belong to any club that would have me as a member"? Yet for all of the neurotic's insecurity, he, too, may harbor an optimism gap. He may deem his own life a mess. But he can still believe that other people's lives are an even bigger mess.

To date, surprisingly little is known about the characteristics of people who flip the I'm OK–They're Not syndrome. Americans who believe that they are failing, yet others are flourishing, are clearly a small proportion of the population. Social scientists have documented that moderately depressed individuals are less likely than other people to exaggerate their own abilities. Unlike most Americans, moderately depressed individuals (though not the severely depressed) have a more accurate reading of reality. They are, as the saying goes, "sadder but wiser."[55]

If Americans' excessive personal optimism often backfires, it can yield dividends, too. The psychoanalyst Otto Rank once observed that "with the truth, one cannot live. To be able to live, one needs illusions."[56] Henrik Ibsen, the famed playwright, got at much the same thought when he wrote, "Rob the average man of his life-illusion, and you rob him also of his happiness."[57] What these writers were suggesting, and what psychologists such as Shelley Taylor and Martin Seligman have documented, is that unrealistic optimism can also work to one's benefit instead of detriment.

In *Positive Illusions* Taylor points out that so-called wishful thinking can be invaluable in helping patients fight off cancer, surmount depression, or muster the courage to take risks—as long as people's optimistic beliefs about their own powers don't become delusional, persisting in the face of evidence that their upbeat assessments are untrue. In his best-seller *Learned Optimism,* Martin Seligman notes a slew of other valuable benefits that accrue to optimists. Optimists, for example, outperform equally talented pessimists at work and in school, and they may even lead longer and healthier lives.[58] The famed placebo effect is perhaps the best-known evidence that individuals will report feeling better simply because they believe they are taking action to help themselves.

While a case can be made that unrealistic optimism is good for people, it is hard to see any lasting benefits to Americans' current pessimism about the state of the country. The next three chapters examine facts that rebut the exaggerated and mistaken claims of American decline that are fostered by the optimism gap. The I'm OK–They're Not syndrome will never vanish, since it is ingrained in human nature. But even though the chasm between private and public expectations cannot be eliminated, it can and must be narrowed for the better for the sake of the nation.

The Myth
of Social
Regression

CHAPTER FOUR

The trouble with this country is
that there are too many people
going about saying "the trouble
with this country is . . ."

SINCLAIR LEWIS[1]

The tenacity of the optimism gap cannot be understood without addressing its central premise head-on: Is America, in fact, in a state of decline? So long as that question goes unanswered, the I'm OK—They're Not syndrome will perpetuate itself. The more voters are convinced the nation is not "OK," the more they will be inclined to ignore or dismiss good news about the country.

To evaluate whether America is declining or advancing, it is necessary to look at whether the nation today is better or worse off in various respects than in the past. Yet the country's political leaders repeatedly duck the compared-to-what question. They are notorious for taking horrifying news stories and transmogrifying them into tales of national atrophy. In 1995, for example, Americans learned of the brutal murder of Deborah Evans and two of her children by three accomplices. One of the accomplices performed a crude C-section on Evans after she died in order to remove a 38-week-old baby whom the alleged murderer claimed for her own.² Was the grisly, bizarre murder unusual?

Not according to Newt Gingrich. Here is how the House Speaker analyzed its meaning in a speech to the Republican Governors Association:

> This is not an isolated incident; there's barbarity after barbarity. There's brutality after brutality. And we shake our heads and say "well, what went wrong?" What's going wrong is the welfare system which subsidized people for doing nothing; a criminal system which tolerated drug dealers; an educational system which allows kids to not learn. . . . And then we end up with the final culmination of a drug-addicted underclass with no sense of humanity, no sense of civilization, and no sense of the rules of life in which human beings respect each other. . . . The child who was killed was endowed by God. And because we aren't willing to say that any more in a public place, and we're not willing to be tough about this any more, and we don't tell four-, five-, and six-year-olds "there are things you can't do, we will not tolerate drug dealing," we then turn around one day and find that we tolerated the decay of our entire civilization. And it's not just violence. In last year's National Assessment of Educational Progress, 74 percent of the fourth-graders could not read at fourth-grade level. . . . A civilization that only has 26 percent of its fourth-graders performing at fourth-grade level is a civilization in danger of simply falling apart.³

It is easy to see that Gingrich exaggerated. As the father of a five-year-old, I do not know any parents who are unwilling to voice their objections to drug dealers to their children. (Certainly, one would be hard-pressed to demonstrate that indifference to the presence of drug dealers is a norm among parents with young children.) But the more telling part of Gingrich's speech was the chain of logic he followed in arguing for American decline. Gingrich began with a horror story and then claimed similar horror stories happened all the time. From there, he assumed something "went wrong" in society, spun out his pet theories about the corrupting welfare state, and eventually ended up with American civilization on the verge of collapse.

What is striking about all this is that Gingrich, the former history professor, makes no reference to history. When Gingrich's claims are placed in context, they evaporate. For example, the reading scores for fourth graders that Gingrich decried were all *lower* a quarter century ago when the NAEP tests began for white, black, and Hispanic students.[4] If the current NAEP scores testify to a civilization in danger of falling apart, think of how endangered American society was a quarter century ago. (Gingrich also botched the test results. The test scores showed that about 60 percent of fourth graders were not "proficient" readers, not that 74 percent of them read below grade level.[5] By definition, 50 percent of those tested read above "grade level.")

Similar questions might be posed about Gingrich's claims about the criminal justice system. Does law enforcement really "tolerate" drug dealers? More drug dealers are locked up, serving longer sentences, today than ever before. That does not mean drug dealing has been halted, but it does not suggest a policy of looking the other way. What about the notion that our streets are marked by barbarity after barbarity? Are Americans significantly more likely to murder each other today than a quarter century ago? Not really. The homicide rate was a hair higher in 1995 than in 1970 (8.2 homicides per 100,000 inhabitants in 1995 versus 7.9 homicides per 100,000 inhabitants in 1970).[6] By 1971, and for the remainder of the 1970s in fact, the homicide rate was substantially *higher* than in 1995.[7]

The Doom-and-Gloom of Pundits, Pols, and the Intelligentsia

Once, presidents exulted in the notion of American progress. With his characteristic bluntness, Harry Truman declared: "There are some people who say that this great Republic of ours is on the way out. They don't know what they are talking about. We are only at the beginning of very great things."[8]

By contrast, Democrats today sound almost apocalyptic when they talk about the future. In 1992, shortly before he became vice president, Al Gore wrote a long book, *Earth in the Balance,* in which he warns that the United States will face inevitable "ecological collapse" unless people start treating threats like global warming and the need for environmental preservation as the organizing principle of humanity.[9] The year before, then–Senate Majority Leader George Mitchell wrote *World on Fire,* in which he announces that the "Four Horsemen" of ecological holocaust—greenhouse warming, ozone layer holes, acid rain, and tropical deforestation—are "killing our water, our air, our plants, our animals, and eventually, if not checked, they will kill us." If Americans do not halt "this deadly quartet now loose on our planet," Mitchell writes, "life as we know it will change dramatically in the twenty-first century, and much of it will end."[10]

President Clinton himself has regularly sounded somber warnings about the status of workers and American families, at least until the 1996 election, when consultants Dick Morris and Mark Penn persuaded Clinton to adopt a more sunny tone in his speeches. Does anyone remember Clinton talking about how the nation was "in a funk"?[11] Or how about his claim in the 1995 State of the Union that "far more than our material riches are [now] threatened; things far more precious to us—our children, our families, our values. . . . The values that used to hold us all together seem to be coming apart. . . . We see our families and our communities all over this country coming apart."[12]

On the political right, Republicans give no quarter to Democrats when it comes to alarmism. During the 1996 campaign, Bob Dole dubbed himself the "most optimistic man in America." But throughout the election, Dole's speeches were laced with doom-and-gloom about the country. In one typical week in February 1996, Dole contended that America was a nation "whose problems seem to grow deeper and deeper every year," that "American parents have never been more worried about their children," and that "these are the worst of times for many who live on Main Street."[13] By the end of the campaign, Dole even made the preposterous claim in a nationally televised debate with Clinton that "we have the worst economy in a century."[14]

To be fair, the rest of the chattering classes—particularly journalists and intellectuals—are often every bit as hyperbolic about the state of the nation as our political leaders. In 1996, the *New York Times,* the gray lady of journalism, published a seven-part series entitled "The Downsizing of America." The story's thesis was that job downsizing was so rampant that the nation was now in the midst of "the most acute job insecurity since the Depression. And this in turn has produced an unrelenting angst that is shattering people's notions of work and self and the very promise of tomorrow."[15] Although a handful of reporters criticized the *Times* series, it won journalism awards. It was very much apace with other news coverage during the post-1992 era, a time when the economy had expanded rapidly, adding millions of new jobs. *U.S. News & World Report,* for example, ran a cover the same year that pictured a group of workers under the headline "Is the American Worker Getting SHAFTED? The Assault of the Middle Class."[16]

For most of the 1990s, various members of the mainstream press indulged in the-sky-is-falling coverage of other areas of

American life that had taken a turn for the better, such as the environment and race. To take one especially dramatic example: TV pundit and syndicated columnist Carl Rowan wrote a book in 1996 titled *The Coming Race War in America*. There he asserts that the United States is in precipitous decline, with the American Dream now "a hellish nightmare."[17] Racism, Rowan claims, "has not been as virulent throughout America since the Civil War." He concludes that a "terrible race war is coming in the United States. It is coming fast."[18]

For all of America's enduring racial problems, it is hard to see how any serious student of history or public attitudes could claim that racism is more virulent today than 30 years ago, much less 50 years ago, when most blacks in the nation still lived in apartheidlike conditions in the South. The black nationalist Marcus Garvey also once predicted that it will be "a terrible day when black men draw the sword to fight for their liberty, and that day is coming . . . the day of the war of the races."[19] Thankfully, time has so far proved Garvey wrong. But Garvey's prediction was made in 1919, when hundreds of thousands of blacks resided in overcrowded shacks that had no plumbing, the Ku Klux Klan was a formidable force throughout the South, one in three blacks could neither read nor write, and most whites in the nation held avowedly racist views. Despite nostalgia for the good ol' days, in 1950 three in four black households lived in substandard housing, and only one in four black families owned a car.[20]

If reporters did not routinely shirk the lessons of history, Rowan's book might be dismissed as goofy. Today, however, his alarmist rhetoric no longer seems extreme. TV commentator Tony Brown's *Black Lies, White Lies,* published shortly before Rowan's book, claims racial problems have reached such a peak that the United States is now "on the path of self-destruction as a nation." *Race Matters,* a 1994 book by Harvard professor Cornel West, states that Americans are now "living in one of the most frightening moments in the history of this country" and concludes that the basic issue confronting black America is *"the nihilistic threat to its very existence."*[21] According to a 1997 poll sponsored by Gannett News Service, such sentiments are not just the beliefs of a radical fringe. A startling 42 percent of Americans agree "with a few recent books that have warned race relations have worsened and the United States may be headed for a race war."[22]

As for the American intelligentsia, it is not altogether surprising that they, too, have overwhelmingly allied themselves in the declinist camp. In his 1997 oeuvre *The Idea of Decline in Western History,* Arthur Herman documents a centuries-long tradition of liberal and conservative intellectuals bemoaning the alleged deterioration of the West. The declinist camp, Herman notes, has taken special root in American soil:

> For the better part of three decades, America's preeminent thinkers and critics—from Norman Mailer, Gore Vidal, Thomas Pynchon, Christopher Lasch, Jonathan Kozol, and Garry Wills to Joseph Campbell, Joan Didion, Susan Sontag, Jonathan Schell, Robert Heilbroner, Richard Sennett, Noam Chomsky, Paul Goodman, Michael Harrington, E. L. Doctorow and Kirkpatrick Sale . . . have advanced a picture of American society . . . [in which it] appears as materialistic, spiritually bankrupt, and devoid of human values. Modern people are always displaced, rootless, psychologically scarred, and isolated from one another. They are, as the Unabomber puts it, "demoralized." The key question now becomes not *if* American society . . . can be saved, but whether it deserves to be saved at all."[23]

If anything, the intelligentsia's doom-and-gloom has become even more marked in recent years. When the *New York Times Magazine* ran an item on new books in 1997 the accompanying headline—"Experts Agree: We're Finished"—was written only half in jest.[24]

Consider just a few of the recent books by conservative luminaries. There is Robert Bork, *Slouching Toward Gomorrah* ("This is a book about American decline. . . . there are aspects of almost every branch of our culture that are worse than ever before and . . . the rot is spreading");[25] Robert Hughes, *Culture of Complaint* ("What Herod saw was America in the late 80s and early 90s . . . [America is] like late Rome . . . in the corruption and verbosity of its senators . . . and in its submission to senile, deified emperors");[26] Samuel Huntington, *The Clash of Civilizations and the Remaking of World Order* ("On a worldwide basis Civilization seems in many respects to be yielding to barbarism, generating the image of an unprecedented phenomenon, a global Dark Ages");[27] Zbigniew Brzezinski, *Out of Control* ("[America] must come to grips with the realization that . . . a community which partakes of no shared absolute certainties but which instead puts a premium on individual self-satisfaction is a community threatened by dissolution");[28] and Edward Luttwak, *The Endangered American Dream* ("If present trends simply continue, all but a small minority of Americans will be impoverished soon enough, left to yearn hopelessly for the lost golden age of American prosperity").[29]

As Herman shows, declinism comes in two basic strains. The conservative and neoconservative version, iterated in the books cited above, is that America is rotting, spoiled by its affluence and permissiveness, engulfed in hedonism, and morally bankrupted. The liberal counterpart is that society is racist, greedy, sexist, homophobic, and so on. Unlike most conservatives, many liberal declinists and Marxists actually *welcome* signs of decay as the prelude to the destruction of the old society and its replacement with a more just order.[30]

Conservative intellectuals, though, are hardly alone these days in foreseeing the end of the American empire. Those on the political left are every bit as gloomy. There is, for example, the legendary environmental doomsayer Paul Ehrlich, who with his wife, Anne, recently wrote *Betrayal of Science and Reason* ("Humanity is now facing a sort of slow-motion environmental Dunkirk").[31] There is Noam Chomsky writing in *The New American Crisis* ("For most of the population, conditions of life and work are grim and declining, something new in the history of industrial society").[32] And there is Jeremy Rifkin, *The End of Work* ("The economic fortunes of most working people continue to deteriorate amid the embarrassment of technological riches").[33]

America-bashing in the academic community has reached enough of a critical mass that scholarly journals have started writing about the phenomenon. A recent issue of *Daedalus,* the highbrow quarterly published by the American Academy of Arts and Sciences, features an article titled simply "Is the United States Falling Apart?"[34] (To the authors' credit, they conclude that it isn't.)

Far more alarmist is a November 1996 symposium in the conservative journal *First Things.* In an editorial headlined "The End of Democracy?" editor in chief Father Richard Neuhaus asks a group of conservative scholars and activists whether the federal courts have so usurped the popular will on issues such as abortion that "conscientious citizens can no longer give moral assent to the existing regime." All that stands between America and Nazi Germany, Neuhaus warns, is "blind hubris."[35]

In response to Neuhaus's query, Robert Bork likens the majority of the Supreme Court to a "band of outlaws."[36] Bork suggests that yes, perhaps it is time to deprive the courts of the right of constitutional review. Charles Colson, the born-again chairman of the Prison Fellowship and former aide to Richard Nixon, frets that the nation is "fast approaching" the point where Christians might feel compelled to organize to resist the government. But it is premature, he concludes, to "advocate open rebellion."[37]

The suggestion by a serious conservative journal that it

might be time to overthrow the U.S. government was a little much, even for some of those on the right who had bemoaned the state of the nation. "I take the demoralization of America quite seriously," William Bennett responds in the January 1997 issue of *First Things*. "But the analogy to Nazi Germany is both wrong and regrettable. . . . we are still America, not 'Amerika.' "[38] So, according to the conservative declinists, America may be badly "demoralized," but thankfully it still has a few remaining ethical tenets that separate it from Nazi Germany and merit our support. That summary of the state of the nation is, of course, absurd. But it illustrates the air of unreality and exaggeration that permeates the discussion of American decline.

The Good News Surprise

Not all of the news about America is good. Yet most of the country's fundamental economic and social trends have improved over the last quarter century. That fact would surprise millions of Americans who feel as though they are living in Babylon.

Given that the Soviet Union has collapsed, that the threat of nuclear annihilation has almost vanished, and that the nation is now inundated with immigrants who cling to rafts, wade, swim, and run to reach our borders, it may seem an odd time to herald the demise of America. Quite apart from the question of America's standing in the world community, however, many domestic indexes have actually improved. In fact, much of what people presume about key social trends in America is wrong. Here are just a few examples at odds with the conventional wisdom:

Crime

Violent crime in the United States appears to be at its lowest level in a quarter century. There are two ways of tracking trends in crime. The first is to examine the Federal Bureau of Investigation's *Uniform Crime Reports,* which tabulate crimes reported to law enforcement agencies from around the nation. The second source of evidence is the Justice Department's annual national victimization surveys, which are huge polls that randomly sample approximately 100,000 people. The victimization surveys cover crimes not reported to police. (Only about a third of all crimes are reported to law enforcement agencies, and this fraction can change over time.) As a result, the victimization surveys are more representative than conventional crime statistics and are favored by many criminologists.

In 1996, violent crime rates were at their lowest levels since the victimization surveys started in 1973. According to the Justice Department reports, violent crime rates peaked 17 years ago, in 1981, and the rates of aggravated assault and rape are now lower than at any time in the previous 23 years.[39] Meanwhile, property crime, which accounts for the bulk of all crime, had also plummeted to its lowest level since the federal surveys began. In 1996, the rates of household theft and burglary were about half of what they had been in 1973.[40] The drop in property crime is so substantial that New York City now has a lower theft and burglary rate than London, and Los Angeles has fewer burglaries than Sydney, Australia.[41]

Victimization surveys have one important gap: They do not track murders, since homicide victims cannot be interviewed after the fact. However, the FBI's *Uniform Crime Reports* do track homicides and the murder totals are considered accurate, because homicide is a crime that is hard to underreport. In 1996, the homicide rate of 7.4 murders per 100,000 inhabitants was well below the peak of 10.2 murders per 100,000 people in 1980.[42] It was, in fact, virtually identical to the homicide rate in 1969, higher than in the 1950s, but lower than in 1931–34.[43] Most of this well-publicized drop in violent crime has been concentrated in the nation's largest cities. In New York and Boston, fewer people were murdered in 1996 than at any time since the 1960s.[44] In Los Angeles, fewer people were murdered in 1997 than in any year since 1977—even though the city now has 700,000 more residents.[45]

A skeptic might ask, What about the endangered black male? The homicide rate for black men has also dropped substantially in recent decades. In 1970, the age-adjusted homicide rate for black males was 82.1 per 100,000 individuals; by 1994, the rate had fallen to 66.2 per 100,000 men.[46] The nonwhite male homicide rate in 1994—while still tragically high—was *lower* than it had been in 1939–41.[47]

Still, the conviction that crime is mushrooming persists. In 1996, Yankelovich Partners asked American adults whether they and members of their family were more likely to be a victim of crime than three years earlier, a period during which both the reported violent crime rates and violent victimization rates fell. Almost 60 percent said they felt less safe than three years ago. Just 17 percent felt their odds of not becoming a crime victim had improved.[48] Similarly, a 1996 *Chicago Tribune* poll found that only 7 percent of voters thought violent crime in the nation had declined in the past five years.[49]

While Americans think that crime is rising, they are also convinced that crime is not that bad in their neighborhood. In 1993, the federal government's American Housing Survey asked more than 50,000 individuals whether there was anything that bothered them about their neighborhood. The list of possible complaints was a long one, and included crime, noise, traffic, litter, people, poor government services, and so on. However, most Americans (63 percent) said their neighborhood had "no problems." Nationwide, just 7 percent of families thought crime was a problem in their neighborhood.[50] The proportion of people identifying crime as a neighborhood problem was higher for central-city blacks (20 percent)[51] and poor families on welfare (also 20 percent).[52] Yet even among the latter two groups, the most common neighborhood problem was "no problem."

Drugs

Annual government surveys show that illicit drug use among the general population is at levels far below those of a decade or more ago. Overall drug use peaked in 1979, when the nation had 25 million users, almost twice the current number. Since 1992, illicit drug use has essentially stabilized but at lower levels. Cocaine use hit its high in 1985, when 3 percent of adults, or 5.7 million Americans, reported they had used cocaine the previous month. By 1996, just 0.8 percent of Americans reported use of cocaine in the past month, and the number of current cocaine users had dropped by almost three-fourths since 1985, to 1.75 million.[53] Among high school seniors, marijuana and LSD use has edged upward since 1992. But student use of marijuana remains well below the levels of the late 1970s and early 1980s, as does the use of most hard drugs. In 1981, 21.7 percent of high school seniors reported using an illicit drug other than marijuana during the month previous to when they were surveyed; in 1997, half as many (10.7 percent) did so. High school seniors were also three times more likely to use cocaine in 1985 than they are today.[54]

Nonetheless, Americans remain convinced that abuse of hard drugs (i.e., heroin, hallucinogens, and cocaine) is a burgeoning national epidemic. A 1995 poll for the Center on Addiction and Substance Abuse at Columbia University found that 73 percent of adult respondents believed hard drug use was a "very serious" national problem, and less than 10 percent thought that hard drug use was declining.[55] However, in their backyards, Americans think drug abuse is much less common. Just 31 percent of adults in the center's poll thought hard drug use was a very serious problem in their own community, and

more than half confessed that they personally didn't know anyone who currently used an illicit drug.[56] The same optimism
gap shows up when people are quizzed about their perceptions
of teen drug abuse. More than 80 percent of teenagers think that
illegal drugs are a major problem for teens across the country.
But two out of three teens believe that drug abuse is a minor
problem or not a problem at all in their local schools.[57]

Scholastic Achievement

Despite much-heralded reports of a nation at educational
risk, high school students today do as well as or slightly better
than their predecessors of the mid-1970s on both aptitude and
achievement tests. As Derek Bok writes in his book *The State of
the Nation*, "Contrary to all the alarmist talk, there are even
some recent signs of modest improvement" in academic achievement.[58]

The case that student aptitude has fallen rests largely on
the fact that Scholastic Aptitude Test (SAT) scores declined between the early 1960s and 1970s and have never fully recovered.
However, there are two reasons why those declines don't mean
that today's students are performing worse than their parents.

First, only about half of all high school seniors take the
SAT each year, and the sample is far from representative. In six
states in 1993, more than 70 percent of high school seniors took
the SAT, but in ten other states less than 10 percent of seniors
did so.[59] Unlike the SAT, the Preliminary Scholastic Aptitude
Test (PSAT) is given to representative samples of high school
juniors. Both the math and verbal PSAT scores have stayed the
same from 1959 to the present.[60]

Second, SAT scores declined in the 1960s partly because
millions of low-income students and minority students, who his-
torically scored lower on the test, started staying in school longer
and taking the SAT in larger numbers. Data from the College
Entrance Examination Board show that when SAT scores are

disaggregated by race, they essentially remain stable for whites from 1976 to 1993 and rise over the same period for blacks, Hispanics, and Native Americans.[61] In fact, scores on achievement tests (as opposed to "aptitude" tests) have mostly risen modestly or remained steady since the 1970s. Student scores on seven of the nine trends tracked by the National Assessment of Educational Progress in reading, science, and mathematics have edged upward to an all-time high.[62]

The fact that students today are more likely to graduate from high school than their parents is also an important sign of progress, since a diploma is a prime requisite for landing a job. In 1970, 55 percent of adults had finished high school; by 1994, 81 percent had.[63] The change among blacks was even more marked. In 1996, the Census Bureau announced a milestone: Black and white students nationally now graduate from high school at roughly the same rate.[64] Yet according to a 1996 Gallup poll, two-thirds of Americans believe the dropout rate rose in the past 25 years.[65]

Most Americans, moreover, are sure the public schools are in academic decline. A 1994 poll for the American Association of School Administrators found 54 percent of the populace believed public schools had declined in the last few years, and just 35 percent believed public schools were improving. Closer to home, the public's beliefs were reversed. Fifty-five percent of parents with a child in public school thought their neighborhood school had improved in the last few years, and only 28 percent saw a decline.[66]

Health

In a 1977 essay, the political scientist Aaron Wildavsky presented a puzzle: "If most people are healthier today than people like themselves have ever been, and if access to medical care now is more evenly distributed among rich and poor, why is there said to be a crisis in medical care that requires massive changes? . . . why, in brief, are we doing better but feeling worse?"[67]

Wildavsky's question still bears pondering. Longevity—perhaps the most basic barometer of well-being—has improved markedly in the last quarter century and is now at a record high.[68] The average life expectancy of a newborn is 76 years today, compared to 71 years in 1970. "I have yet to run into an American over the age of 47 who regularly observes 'You know, if I had been born in the nineteenth century, I'd very probably be dead by now,'" observes political scientist John Mueller. "Nobody really thinks in such terms, yet the statement is completely true."[69] Similarly, you don't hear many 70-year-olds today saying, "You know, if I was my age a quarter century ago, I'd probably have one foot in the grave by now."

The infant mortality rate in the United States has also dropped to its lowest level ever.[70] In 1970, black and white babies were twice as likely to die before their first birthday as they are at present.[71] The drop in the number of infants who die is especially telling because infant mortality is a kind of bellwether of good health habits, such as eating properly, abstaining from drugs and smoking, and having regular contact with a pediatrician.

Many more Americans are driving automobiles today and working, yet fatalities from car collisions and workplace accidents have plummeted since 1970.[72] The percentage of Americans who smoke cigarettes has dropped by roughly a quarter since 1974, too.[73] Meanwhile, low-income families are much more likely to have access to health care than in the past.[74]

Ironically, improvements in health care may themselves be a cause of Americans "doing better but feeling worse." As Edward Tenner points out in Why Things Bite Back, "The safer life imposes an ever-increasing burden of attention. . . . people may feel sicker today because they are more likely to survive with some limitation or chronic illness. But they really are better off."[75]

Race

In the last quarter century, the black middle class has mushroomed. In 1996, black median family income, adjusted for inflation, was at an all-time high,[76] and black poverty[77] and infant mortality rates had edged downward to an all-time low.[78] In 1970, about 1 out of every 17 blacks in the 25- to 34-year-old age group had earned a four-year college degree. By 1994, 1 in 8 had done so.[79]

Orlando Patterson, a left-leaning Harvard sociologist, summarizes the import of these shifts in his 1997 book *The Ordeal of Integration*. "African Americans," he writes, "from a condition of mass illiteracy fifty years ago, are now among the most educated groups of people in the world, with median years of schooling and college completion rates higher than those of most European nations. Although some readers may think this observation is a shocking overstatement, it is not."[80] Patterson, who is black, suggests that the "the strange tendency to more loudly lament the black predicament the better it gets can be understood as a paradox of desegregation. . . . as individuals in both groups meet more and more, the possibility for conflict is bound to increase."[81]

As Patterson acknowledges, a minority of blacks in urban ghettos have fared disastrously in the last 25 years. But the big picture is inescapable: Most blacks have prospered, and overt white racism has dramatically declined since the 1960s. Overwhelming majorities of whites today support the principle of equal treatment for the races in schools, jobs, housing, and other public spheres.[82] Interracial friendships and marriages have blossomed as well. In 1970, just 2.6 percent of all new marriages involving an African-American mate were interracial marriages; today, more than 12 percent are interracial unions.[83] Whites' greater openness to interracial marriages is one of the more dramatic attitudinal shifts in the last 25 years. In 1972, only a quarter of whites approved of marriages between blacks and whites. (In 1958, just 4 percent did so.) By 1997, however, over 60 percent of whites approved of interracial marriages.[84]

The conservative magazine *Commentary* suggests that 50 years ago the United States was "confident in its democratic purposes and serene in the possession of a common culture," while now it is "moving toward balkanization or even breakdown."[85] But in the postwar "debalkanized" era, Jim Crow segregation prevailed in schools, buses, restaurants, and other public facilities in the South. Racism was the *norm* among whites. Roughly two in three southern whites felt blacks were not as intelligent as whites. Nationwide, less than half the white populace believed that blacks should have as good a chance as whites to obtain jobs.[86]

Without doubt, there has been a fundamental shift in attitudes during the last half century. Even so, about three-quarters of Americans still believe that racial discrimination against blacks in the United States is a very serious or somewhat serious problem. They don't, however, think discrimination against blacks is a serious problem in the community where they reside. Two in three Americans say discrimination in their area is not too serious or not a problem at all.[87]

White Americans also believe that other whites harbor lots of prejudice, while they themselves are models of tolerance. When a Gallup poll asked some 3,000 adults in 1997 to grade how prejudiced they were against blacks on a scale of 0 to 10, 27 percent of whites said they had absolutely no prejudice (a "0" score), and 36 percent gave themselves a low rating of 1 or 2. Just 14 percent of whites gave themselves a high prejudice score of 5 or higher. When asked, however, to grade *other* whites' prejudice toward blacks on the 0 to 10 scale, whites gave 44 percent of their race a high prejudice score, triple their own self-ratings.[88]

The Limits of Progress

The fact that racial attitudes have improved does not mean that it's time to adopt a don't-worry-be-happy attitude toward the state of America. Despite the economic advances blacks have made, far too many blacks remain entrenched in ghettos. Similarly, it's worth remembering that America still has a high rate of violent crime and a serious drug problem. Many of the nation's public schools are mediocre at best, most inner-city schools are dismal, and one can argue that schools in general have not improved fast enough to keep up with the demands of a more technological economy. As President Clinton put it in a speech during the last campaign: "The crime rate is down, the welfare rolls are down, the food stamp rolls are down, the teen pregnancy rate is down. . . . and yet, we all know that all those things that are going down are still too high."[89]

Even so, the claim that the nation is not advancing as rapidly as it should is quite different from the claim that the country is regressing. Most of the social trends that voters assume are worsening have, in fact, taken a turn for the better over the last quarter century. That should be cause for real optimism.[90] Go back to the 1950s, and all the social trends tracked in the preceding pages—except for crime and drugs—compare even more unfavorably to the present-day situation than in 1970. The average American died years earlier, infants were four times as likely to die before their first birthday, millions more students dropped out of high school or never went on to college, and blacks and women had a smidgen of the opportunities they currently enjoy. Those who prefer to see the glass at present as half-empty should at least concede that it was never much fuller in the past. The good ol' days weren't so good after all.[91]

The Myth
of Moral
Decline

CHAPTER FIVE

If its individual citizens, to a man,
are to be believed, [America] always
is depressed, and always is stagnated,
and always is at an alarming crisis,
and never was otherwise.

CHARLES DICKENS[1]

Shortly after World War II, the British social critic and journalist Malcolm Muggeridge came to the United States for the first time as the Washington correspondent for the *Daily Telegraph*. Americans then had good cause for optimism. The worst war in world history was over, America had emerged as the most powerful nation on the planet, and returning veterans by the millions were attending college and purchasing subsidized houses under the GI Bill. The Marshall Plan, perhaps the most bighearted rebuilding effort ever launched to aid foreign allies, was still some months away. However, Muggeridge was unimpressed by America. "The whole show is a fraud," he wrote. "The appalling melancholia induced by this country is due to the fact that the light of the spirit is quite out, making a kingdom of darkness."[2]

Muggeridge's despair, for all it may have been exaggerated then, sounds quite ordinary today. Many Americans think the light of the spirit is now flickering in the country and could soon be snuffed out. In *Earth in the Balance,* Al Gore writes that "there is indeed a spiritual crisis in modern civilization that seems to be based on an emptiness at its center and the absence of a larger spiritual purpose."[3] Of course, decrying the moral condition of the country is not new; in fact, it is something of an American tradition. But the depth and scope of people's gloom seem more sweeping today than a quarter century ago.[4] An overwhelming majority of voters—around 80 percent in most surveys—feel that the moral and ethical standards of Americans are deteriorating.[5] And this alleged decline of virtue is tied closely to the one unofficial institution that, indisputably, has grown weaker in the last quarter century: the family.

The Family Values Conundrum

Since 1970, divorce and out-of-wedlock childbearing have sky-rocketed in the United States. Many single-parent families manage to flourish, but on average, children raised by single parents are more likely than children raised by both their biological parents to be poor, drop out of school, become pregnant while in their teens, go to juvenile correction facilities, and be unemployed as adults.

Boyfriends and stepparents are also far more likely to abuse or neglect children than are their biological parents.[6] Child abuse and neglect rose in the late 1980s due, most likely, to an increase in single parenthood and the advent of crack cocaine. A report for the Department of Health and Human Services indicates that between 1986 and 1993 the incidence of child abuse in the nation almost doubled.[7] Some of this rise appears to result from definition-creep, with professionals who work with children now readier to classify them as in danger of physical harm or subject to emotional abuse. Most experts believe there has been a real upsurge in the incidence of seriously injured children, too.[8]

Much of the public assumes that Americans' values must be deteriorating as long as family breakdown is on the rise. What does it matter, the argument goes, if a family is less likely to be burglarized today than a quarter century ago if Dad isn't around to offer Johnny daily guidance?

Unquestionably, the high incidence of divorce and out-of-wedlock childbearing has often damaged children and made it harder for some parents to lend emotional support or instill respect for authority. Yet many Americans, laypeople and scholars alike, exaggerate the consequences of family breakdown. The crude one-to-one correlation that exists in public discussion— more kids born out of wedlock automatically equals higher crime rates, weaker moral standards, worse schools, sicker children, and so on—has not been borne out in recent years. Crime rates have dropped, scholastic achievement has stabilized or edged upward, and infant mortality has declined, even as the out-of-wedlock birth ratio has risen. Nor is it clear that the ethical standards of Americans have declined.

Here again, when members of the public voice their distress about family breakdown, they are almost always referring to *other* people's families, not their own. Since 1989, the Massachusetts Mutual Life Insurance Company has sponsored an annual national survey of Americans' views of family and family values. The report on the 1995 survey, prepared by Michaels Opinion Research, summarized the findings of the earlier polls as follows:

> One of the ongoing contradictions revealed in [the surveys] is the consistent tendency of the public to transfer many of the perceived problems in U.S. society to other citizens. . . . [Americans believe that] values in society are going downhill, but within my

family, values are important and strong. Family life in the U.S. is not good, but I'm very satisfied with the quality of my family life. A lack of commitment is a major problem for society, but I'm having little difficulty meeting commitments to my family.[9]

Americans aren't just pleased with their own family life; they are delighted. In a 1997 Mother's Day survey, the Pew Research Center found that 93 percent of mothers with kids under 18 felt their children were a source of happiness all or most of the time; 90 percent said their marriage made them happy all or most of the time; and just 2 percent of moms reported being dissatisfied with the job they were doing rearing their children.[10] In poll after poll, less than 10 percent of Americans say they are worse parents than were their own parents, and compared to the moms and dads of twenty years ago, today's parents are actually much more likely to rate traditional values, such as hard work, religion, patriotism, and having children as being "very important."[11] In their own lives, three out of four adults don't find it difficult to meet their commitments to their families, kids, and employers—even though 90 percent also believe that a "major problem with society" is that people don't live up to their commitments.[12]

To ensure that respondents were not just glossing over problems in their own families, the Michaels firm added several questions in their 1995 survey to probe the personal consequences of the perceived national decline in values. One question inquired how the decline in values "directly affected the quality of your life" and provided respondents with 20 possible examples from which to pick. The respondents still didn't feel the decline in values affected them personally. In fact, the most frequently cited response from people was that they were either "not affected" at all by deteriorating values (32 percent) or couldn't think of an example of how they had been affected (12 percent).

A third of those surveyed in 1995 did allow that, compared to 10 years ago, they were having a somewhat difficult or very difficult time keeping their lives in harmony with their values. However, even when people who admitted they were struggling were asked why they felt that way, they didn't primarily cite marital difficulties, problems with kids, or financial setbacks. Instead, the chief explanation for their discordant lives was— surprise!—a "decline in national values."[13]

Americans may fret over the decline of the family, but they evidence surprisingly little interest in boosting parental commitment, especially when doing so might restrict their personal freedoms. Until the late 1960s, couples wanting to divorce had to demonstrate that their spouses had seriously wronged them through adultery, extreme cruelty, desertion, a stint in prison, or a similar offense. As a result, millions of couples stayed together in strained and sometimes abusive marriages. The no-fault divorce law revolution of the 1970s made it possible for couples to divorce on much milder grounds—such as incompatibility or irreconcilable differences—without the consent of their spouse.

Since 1974, roughly 40 to 50 percent of adults have said that divorce should be more difficult to obtain. But when bills to toughen or overturn no-fault divorce laws come before state legislatures—which are usually peppered with divorced lawmakers—they typically start off with a burst of publicity and end up being quietly shelved.[14]

The essential paradox is that while Americans believe today's moral breakdown was spawned by the permissiveness of the 1960s, they embrace, on a case-by-case basis, most of the liberties that were part of the 1960s revolution. When Americans are asked, as they were in a 1996 *Wall Street Journal* poll, what kind of impact various social movements have had on today's values, they almost invariably think they are beneficial. Roughly 80 percent of those surveyed by the *Journal* said that the civil rights movement, the environmental movement, and the women's movement all had a positive impact on people's values.[15]

The previous year, the Gallup Organization also quizzed members of the public about whether they thought various changes had been good or bad for society. Hefty majorities of Americans thought the greater openness today toward divorced people was good for society, as was the greater openness about sex and the human body, changes in the role of women, greater cultural and ethnic diversity, the increased willingness to question government authority, and the greater attention paid to equality for racial and ethnic minorities. In only one instance (society's increased acceptance of homosexuality) did most people think social change had harmed society.[16]

If policymakers could somehow reverse the various social movements that voters now endorse, they would create a society like—well, like America in the 1950s. Divorce would be less common, premarital sex would be rarer, blacks and women would have less opportunity to succeed in the job market, and manufacturers could pollute the environment with relative impunity. Americans consistently pick the 1950s as the decade that they most would like to have grown up in.[17] Yet if they were actually flashed back to the 1950s in a time tunnel, many people would find the era oppressive. Put another way, most Americans believe the social movements of the present day are a testament to progress, not decline.

By All That's Holy

The problem of "family breakdown" can be thought of as a surrogate Rorschach test. Voters hear of its poignant consequences among divorced friends, or see news stories about latchkey kids and crack babies, and before long, every problem starts looking as though it can ultimately be traced back to family breakdown. One might, for example, infer that organized religion is slipping if out-of-wedlock childbearing and single-parenting are mushrooming. In fact, three in four Americans believe the nation is in spiritual decline.[18] Yet the sway of organized religion is much greater in the United States today than in most Western nations, and the religiosity of Americans is at near record levels.

As Seymour Martin Lipset, a neoconservative intellectual, sums up in his 1996 book *American Exceptionalism,* "The historical evidence indicates that religious affiliation and belief in America are much higher in the twentieth century than in the nineteenth, and have not decreased in the post–World War II era. . . . The standard evidence marshalled to argue that America is experiencing a value crisis is unconvincing."[19] Such counterconventional claims are hard for members of the public to accept, again, because of the optimism gap. Two-thirds of the electorate think that religion is losing its influence on American life. Yet 62 percent say that religion's influence is increasing in their own lives, according to a 1994 *U.S. News & World Report* poll.[20]

Today, a solid majority of Americans belong to churches and synagogues, much as they have since the 1930s, when scientific polling began. In 1997, 68 percent of Americans reported belonging to a church or synagogue,[21] not much below the 73 percent who said they belonged in both 1965 and 1952.[22] Some members of the clergy have asserted that these high levels of church membership conceal a dip in religious commitment and belief. It's true that weekly attendance at religious services was "only" 41 percent in 1997.[23] This was down a bit from its peak in 1958, when 49 percent of Americans said they had attended services the previous week. But attendance in 1997 was very similar to attendance in 1950, when 39 percent of Americans said they had attended a service the previous week.[24] In 1997, the Gallup poll replicated one of its surveys on Americans' religious practices from 1947. The fifty-year update found that the same percentage of Americans pray today (90 percent), believe in God (96 percent), and attend church once a week. About the only difference between the two eras was that Americans were actually more likely to give grace or give thanks aloud in 1997 than in 1947 (63 percent compared to 43 percent).[25]

George Gallup, Jr., summarizes the evidence by observing that "the religious beliefs and practices of Americans today look very much like those of the 1930s and 1940s. The percent of the populace who are active church members today closely matches the figures recorded in the 1930s."[26] Nor is it the case, as Roger Finke and Rodney Stark point out in their influential book *The Churching of America, 1776–1990,* that acceptance of traditional religious doctrine is down. Most Americans still say that religion is central to their own lives: Roughly 60 percent of adults think that religion "can answer all or most of today's problems," and one in three view at least one religious TV show each week. After reviewing church membership records and other historical evidence, Finke and Stark conclude that "to the degree that denominations rejected traditional doctrines and ceased to make serious demands on their followers, they ceased to prosper. The churching of America was accomplished by aggressive churches committed to vivid otherworldliness."[27]

The Ethics "Crisis"

Conceivably, the nation could still be in moral decline even when its citizens claim to be deeply religious. A skeptic might suggest that Americans are simply bigger hypocrites than ever. In 1993, Everett Carll Ladd, the president of the Roper Center for Public Opinion Research, attempted to assess that proposition by examining whether the unethical behavior of Americans had risen in recent decades. In an article titled "The Myth of Moral Decline," Ladd reports his findings: There is no compelling evidence that Americans' moral conduct or ethical standards are slipping, but ever since the introduction of polling in the mid-1930s, most Americans have felt moral standards were in decline.[28] In 1963, for instance, only a third of all adults said they were satisfied "with the honesty and standards of behavior of people in the country today."[29]

Ladd acknowledges there is abundant evidence that large numbers of modern-day Americans err and sin. Yet in tracking trends over time, there is little proof that the moral state of the country's citizenry has deteriorated. Philanthropic giving as a percentage of personal income declined slightly between 1969 and 1972 but has essentially remained steady ever since. However, because Americans' personal incomes have risen substantially since the 1950s, individual citizens are now donating more money to charities than their parents did, even after accounting for inflation.[30] Volunteering seems to have become *more* common. When the Gallup poll first queried people in 1977 about their participation in charitable and social service activities that aid the poor, the sick, and the elderly, a quarter of the populace said they participated. By 1994, that number had doubled to almost half of all adults.[31]

News stories about citizens who evade paying their taxes suggest that more Americans cheat on their taxes today than in the past. Yet the Internal Revenue Service thinks that compliance with the tax code has risen modestly in recent decades. Since 1973, the IRS has tracked the "voluntary compliance rate," a number that describes the percentage of their total tax liability that individuals and corporations pay voluntarily. The voluntary compliance rate for the individual income tax was roughly 83 percent in 1992, a hair higher than in 1973. The rate for the corporate income tax was similar, and it too had edged up slightly.[32]

It is an article of faith among educators that cheating has exploded in recent decades, but here again the evidence is mixed. Ladd notes that in 1959, 86 percent of high school students told Gallup pollsters that there was a "great deal" or a "fair amount" of cheating at their own schools; by 1992, only 55 percent reported that much cheating. The percentage of students saying they themselves had cheated has also dropped substantially, from 62 percent in 1978 to 46 percent in 1992.[33] Surveys of high school students in central and northern Georgia in 1969, 1979, and 1989 show that the number of students reporting that they had used cheat sheets on tests and had let others copy their work rocketed from 1969 to 1979 and then edged upward a bit from 1979 to 1989. However, the proportion of students who said they had turned in work done by another student or by their parents remained unchanged during the two-decade span.[34]

Trends in college cheating are ambiguous, too. A 1993 study by Donald McCabe and Linda Klebe Trevino of Rutgers University replicated a 1963 analysis of cheating at nine state universities. In an article in *Change* magazine, McCabe and Trevino reported that "the dramatic upsurge in cheating heralded by the media was not found." Their study did find that cheating on tests and exams increased from 1963 to 1993. But they also discovered that serious cheating on written work, such as plagiarism and turning in work done by others, had declined slightly. Somewhat surprisingly, the increase in test cheating was largely confined to women, far more of whom were competing with men in majors such as business, engineering, and science, where students were more likely to cheat.[35] Ladd himself concludes: "Has there in fact been a deterioration in moral conduct in the United States, as compared to, say, the 1950s? . . . [The] available information is inconclusive or flat-out says otherwise."[36]

One possible explanation for why Americans are convinced their fellow citizens' morals have declined is that they feel less connected to their communities and fellow citizens than a quarter century ago. In his much-debated "Bowling Alone" essay,

Harvard professor Robert Putnam points out that membership in traditional civic organizations, such as the Parent-Teacher Association (PTA) and the Boy Scouts, as well as membership in fraternal groups, such as the Lions, Elks, and Jaycees, has dropped substantially in the last quarter century.[37]

During the same time period, membership in professional organizations, mass-membership groups, and self-help organizations (e.g., the American Association of Retired Persons, the Sierra Club, and Alcoholics Anonymous) rose. But Putnam argues that these latter groups require little from their members besides a dues check and seldom build lasting community ties. Putnam drew the title of his controversial article from the fact that while more Americans are bowling than ever before, fewer Americans are bowling in organized leagues.

Critics like journalists Robert Samuelson and Nicholas Lemann, as well as scholars like Ladd and Michael Schudson, have pointed out that Putnam's selective use of data seriously exaggerates the extent of civic decline.[38] Still, time-diary studies in which people keep track of their activities from minute to minute show that Americans now spend less time socializing than 30 years ago, with most of their added leisure time spent watching television instead. In 1965, people spent about an extra hour a week—or more than two full days a year—socializing with friends and attending parties than in 1985.[39] If Americans' sense of neighborliness and traditional forms of civic engagement have declined somewhat, people could well feel more isolated and mistrustful of others than in the recent past. That mistrust may help explain why so many Americans feel "other" people's moral conduct is deteriorating—even though there is little evidence that the kingdom of darkness has descended upon us.

The Myth of Economic Decline

CHAPTER SIX

A house may be large or small; as long as the surrounding houses are equally small it satisfies all social demands for a dwelling. But if a palace rises beside the little house, the little house shrinks to a hut.

KARL MARX[1]

While conservatives have championed the claim that America is in a period of social regression and moral decline, liberals have promulgated another declinist myth: that the average worker's living standards have fallen since the OPEC-driven recession of 1973–75. As a result, the poor are getting poorer, and the baby boom generation is having a harder time making ends meet and attaining the American middle-class dream than their parents did. "People are working harder for less," as President Clinton has succinctly put it.[2]

The notion that workers are worse off falls on a receptive electorate, which, in keeping with the I'm OK–They're Not syndrome, displays a deep-seated resistance to good news about the economy. Every week, from December 1985 until the present, ABC News and *Money* magazine have asked national samples of voters whether they would describe the state of the economy as "excellent, good, not so good, or poor." More than 500 times in a row, more voters labeled the economy not so good to poor than tagged it good to excellent—even though the economy plainly expanded from 1986 to 1989 and from 1992 to 1997. In 1995, after three years of economic growth, half of all Americans actually thought the country was in a recession.[3] It was not until a week after the November 1996 election—for the first time in almost 11 years—that a majority of respondents said the economy was good to excellent.[4]

The Mirage of Falling Living Standards

The liberals' case for the decline in living standards rests on three large, disturbing facts: Since 1973, the real hourly earnings of workers have fallen (about 15 percent by 1993), median family income has also fallen (about 12 percent by 1992), and income inequality has grown dramatically.[5] These shifts seem stark, compared to the post–World War II era, when wages and family income rose steadily.

Yet as damning as these numbers are, they are specious. They do not demonstrate that living standards are slipping, the chief reason being that they fail to provide an apples-to-apples comparison of how Americans are faring. For example, families are smaller today than they were in 1973, so they need less income to maintain the same living standard.[6] Fringe benefits have risen substantially since 1973 and now are an important part of what people "earn"—but are not reflected in wage trends.[7] (The percentage of workers with employer-provided health care coverage has dropped since 1979,[8] but business contributions to 401(k) plans have mushroomed during the same time period.) Age matters, too; when an unusually large cohort of young adults enter the labor market, they naturally start out in lower-wage jobs and then move on to better-paying positions later in their careers. To evaluate whether today's parents are faring worse than their parents, we should compare their economic status with that of their parents at a similar age.

Finally, properly adjusting wages and income for inflation makes a difference. The numbers cited above are deflated by the consumer price index. The CPI, however, certainly overstated inflation prior to 1983 and, in the view of most economists, still overstates it today. A 1996 report to the Senate Finance Committee from an advisory commission of economists chaired by Michael Boskin concluded that the CPI overstated inflation by 1.1 points per annum in recent years.[9] (Some economists, however, think this estimate may be too high.)

Over two decades, even a small overestimate of inflation can make a large difference. If the CPI overstated inflation each year by 1.1 points from 1973 to 1995, the reported 13-percent decline in real hourly earnings during that time would actually amount to an increase of 13 percent. By the same token, real median income would have risen 36 percent from 1973 to 1995, not the measly 4 percent reported in official statistics.[10]

A simpler, less controversial approach than the Boskin commission's is to use an alternative index developed by the Census Bureau, known as the CPI-U-X1, to take account of the agreed-upon fact that the CPI overstated inflation before 1983. Once adjustments using the CPI-U-X1 and other apples-to-apples comparisons are made, the picture of declining or stagnating living standards shifts to one of modest betterment. Median family income, adjusted for changes in family size, rose 9 percent from 1973 to 1992. After fringe benefits are accounted for, real hourly compensation (i.e., wages plus benefits) rose 15 percent from 1973 to 1993.[11]

Such increases tend to go unnoticed because they come with a price tag: More and more women feel obliged to work outside the home to ensure that their family maintains a middle-class standard of living. This is necessary because, as Robert Samuelson points out, "today's middle-class lifestyle is a lot richer" than it was in the 1970s or in the 1950s. If "people want to duplicate their parents' lifestyles," writes Samuelson, "they can unplug their air conditioners, sell one of their cars, discard their VCRs and PCs and stop sending all their kids to college."[12]

Is it a positive or negative development that millions of women have shifted from housework to work at an office? A case can be made either way, and women themselves are evenly divided on the issue. Asked in a 1994 Roper Starch poll whether they would of their own free choice prefer to have a job outside the home or stay home to take care of a house and family, 47 percent of women opted for staying home and 46 percent opted for working.[13] More recent surveys confirm that many working women would prefer to put in shorter hours or fewer days each week. But relatively few of them—just 17 percent in one 1997 poll—would like to stop working altogether, even if they could maintain the same standard of living without working. Contrary to popular wisdom, working moms also tend to be more satisfied with their lives than mothers who don't work.[14]

Yet no matter where one comes down on the question of working mothers, the average American is better off in sheer dollar terms than in the past. Consider, for example, the economist's standard yardstick for gauging changes in living standards, per capita disposable income. It measures how much income the average person has to spend after taxes. According to the 1998 *Economic Report to the President,* real per capita disposable income rose from $13,566 in 1973 to a record high of $19,331 in 1997.[15]

In layperson's terms, that means Americans, on average, had about 40 percent more money to spend in 1997 than in 1973. Demonstrating again the truth of C. Northcote Parkinson's law—expenditure rises to meet income—Americans spent more, too. Consumption per capita rose 51 percent in real terms, from $11,950 in 1973 to $18,046 in 1997.[16]

Pundits and politicians routinely make statements to the effect that after accounting for inflation, "60 percent of workers haven't had a pay raise in two decades." During the 1996 Republican primaries, Pat Buchanan often claimed that "the vast majority of middle Americans are seeing their standard of living going down."[17] But Buchanan, as well as other politicians and reporters, mixes up two sets of figures. The first set of numbers, which document the upward mobility of workers, is the one the public really cares about. The mobility figures present a longitudinal or moving picture, showing how the wages of *individual workers* are rising or falling over time. The second set of numbers, which are chiefly of interest to economists, provides a cross-sectional snapshot of American workers. It shows how the overall *distribution* of wages among workers has shifted from decade to decade.

Between 1973 and 1993, the overall *distribution* of wages did shift downward. Real hourly wages for the bottom 60 percent of workers in the United States in 1973 were lower than in 1993.[18] But the bottom 60 percent of wage earners in 1973 was not composed of the same people who were in the bottom 60 percent in 1993. In fact, the distribution of wages among workers can shift downward over time, even though the workers who initially started off in lower-income quintiles are *all* receiving steady wage hikes. This seeming contradiction can occur when beginning workers start at lower and lower wages but all workers get small annual raises.[19]

The *distribution* of wages can be depressed for many reasons, some of them quite healthy. The wage distribution will shift downward when lots of new workers enter the job market abruptly (as women started to do in the late 1970s), when more workers are holding part-time jobs (another shift speeded by the entry of women into the job market), when a large wave of unskilled immigrants enter the United States (as occurred in the 1980s and 1990s), or when an unusually large cohort of young workers go looking for the first jobs (read the baby boomers, who entered the labor market in massive numbers from 1965 to 1985). To understand whether workers' wages are rising—and whether they are faring better or worse than their predecessors—it is necessary to trace the wage history of individual workers over time.

During the past two decades, the rate of upward mobility among workers has essentially remained constant;[20] adjusted for inflation, the wages of most workers rise substantially until they reach the age of 55, when their careers start to taper off.[21] America was, and remains, a nation that provides substantial opportunities for advancement. A longitudinal analysis that traced the fate of individual workers by Boston College economist Peter Gottschalk showed that only about a third of those in the bottom fifth of earnings in 1974 were still in the bottom fifth in 1991. The vast majority of working-class and middle-class Americans enjoyed substantial salary raises during that time. By 1991, 20 percent of those in the bottom fifth of earners had moved up to the top quintile of earners.[22]

If anything, the economic playing field may have become slightly more level since the 1970s, with children from less privileged backgrounds more able to move beyond their roots than before. Isabel Sawhill, a former Clinton appointee, coauthored a study of intergenerational mobility in 1997 that concluded, "Class may still matter in the United States, but not as much as it used to. The effect of parents' occupational status on that of their offspring declined by about one-third in less than a generation, according to one study. . . . other studies have confirmed this decline."[23]

Compared to their parents' generation, most people today in their prime working years end up making significantly more than the preceding generation did—and it's not just conservative apologists who make that claim. A study by researchers John Sabelhaus of the Urban Institute and Joyce Manchester of the Congressional Budget Office compared the income and consumption of baby boomers in 1989 with that of their parents' generation in 1960. They found that, on a per adult basis, the baby boomers' income was 55 percent higher than their parents', adjusted for inflation and age.[24] One important part of the American Dream—owning your own house—did dim during the 1980s, as home ownership among younger, married couples declined. Even so, the overall home ownership rate in 1997 (66 percent) was the highest ever,[25] chiefly because of a rise in home ownership among older couples.[26]

Another commonsense benchmark for assessing living standards is to ask about their costs in terms of time: Does it take more time or less time today for the average American worker to pay off a house, car, refrigerator, and other purchases than it did in the past? In fact, the amount of time the typical worker has to put in on the job in order to buy a stove, dishwasher, refrigerator, washing machine, clothes dryer, air conditioner, color television, and house has fallen since 1970 (and has plummeted since the 1950s). To take one example, workers taking home the average hourly wage for production and nonsupervisory workers in manufacturing would have to put in 22 hours on the job to pay for a kitchen range in 1997, 113 hours to pay for the range in 1970, and 345 hours in 1950.[27] With the important exception of the time costs of a college education (and, as it turns out, candy bars), Americans can pay off their purchases with less time on the job today than in the 1970s or 1950s.[28]

Behind all of these dry statistics lie some real improvements in the lifestyle of the average American. To be sure, some of the rise in consumer consumption since the 1973 oil bust is of marginal value. As the liberal economist Paul Krugman sardonically observed, "During the first postwar generation, nearly everyone acquired a telephone; during the second, some of us got call waiting."[29] Yet not all the material improvements in Americans' lives since the 1970s are trivial.

By 1994, consumers spent more money on personal computers than on color televisions.[30] Though still in its infancy, the computer revolution is already changing the way that millions of children learn and adults communicate. Forty percent of American households now have a PC.[31] About two-thirds of the nation's public schools are currently linked up to the Internet,[32] and by 1996, half of the nation's college freshmen used personal computers frequently, nearly double the proportion who did so a decade earlier.[33] Similarly, developments such as E-mail are reducing the isolation of tens of thousands of handicapped Americans and enabling scores of adults to work out of their homes and cut back frequent commutes to work.[34]

Housing conditions have improved for families, too. In 1970, 29 percent of American children lived in overcrowded conditions, a figure that fell to 16 percent by 1990.[35] Modern amenities have proliferated. By 1990, 67 percent of children resided in homes with two or more automobiles, up from 45 percent in 1970.[36] The percentage of households with either central air or room air conditioners—no small concern for the elderly or for families in hot climates—rose from 48 percent in 1973 to 75 percent in 1995.[37] Options that were once largely the province of the well-to-do have opened up for the middle class. In 1972,

Americans took 54 million trips by plane. By 1993, the number had quadrupled, to 222 million trips.[38]

Despite periodic hand-wringing, few Americans would really be surprised by the ongoing rise in people's living standards. In their 1998 book *Attitudes Toward Economic Inequality,* pollster Everett Carll Ladd and researcher Karlyn Bowman report that "when people are asked to compare themselves to their parents, virtually every question we have been able to locate finds that majorities, usually strong ones, say that they are better off today—better off in terms of opportunity, preparation for adulthood, standard of living, quality of life, finances, income, homes, and lifestyle and material possessions—no matter how the question is asked."[39]

Specious Statistics and the Rich-Poor Gap

While Americans believe they have made material progress, most of the public—about 80 percent—is also convinced the rich got richer and the poor got poorer in recent years.[40] As is often the case with the conventional wisdom, it is half right. The rich have tended to get richer. But the poor, at least poor families with children, haven't gotten poorer. That conclusion is at odds with official statistics, which show a large increase in child poverty from 1973 to 1994 (14.4 percent of children lived below the poverty line in 1973; 20.5 percent did in 1996),[41] as well as a sharp decline in real income for families with children at the bottom of the U.S. income distribution.[42] However, the official numbers are misleading, because they are based on annual incomes reported by the poor.

A 1995 study coauthored by Harvard sociologist Christopher Jencks and Susan Mayer of the University of Chicago methodically dismantles the claim that poor children are getting poorer. Jencks, a prominent liberal thinker, reports what many economists know but is little appreciated by members of the public: Namely, the poorest families in the United States spend far more each year than the total income they report receiving. In 1988–89, the poorest fifth of households with children reported a mean income of $9,822, but the same group of families acknowledged spending an average of $16,939 a year. The disparity between reported income and actual consumption grew even more exaggerated after 1973.[43]

In part, reported income is understated because the poor often receive in-kind aid, such as food stamps, that is not counted as income in the official poverty count. On average, food stamps provided about 16 percent of the total family income of poor children in 1989.[44] But the chief explanation for the income-consumption disparity is that many poor families underreport their true incomes. To remain eligible for welfare benefits and to reduce potential tax liability, parents in poor families often conceal money from authorities that they earn from odd jobs or receive from relatives and friends.

When members of the public talk about the poor getting poorer, they are assuming that indigent families today are facing greater material hardships than in earlier decades. Jencks and Mayer, however, found that "the material conditions of life among low-income children mostly either improved or remained unchanged between 1970 and 1990."[45]

In fact, a recent Census Bureau report shows that by 1993, more than 90 percent of officially poor families had a color television, a little more than 70 percent had their own washing machines, and 60 percent had VCRs and microwaves.[46] Poor families in the United States are more likely to have these modern amenities than is the average resident in most Western European nations today or the typical U.S. resident 25 years ago.[47]

Those facts do not demonstrate, as some conservatives have claimed, that material deprivation and poverty have been eradicated in the United States. Roughly 40 percent of poor families have rats, mice, or roaches in their dwellings, and impoverished

Americans are still far more likely than nonpoor Americans to lack the money to pay the rent, to skip getting needed medical attention, to have their utilities turned off, and to go without food for a day.[48] Compared to the poor of a generation ago, however, material hardship has plainly declined, and access to medical care has improved. In 1970, 27 percent of children in the poorest families had not visited a doctor in the previous 12 months. By 1989, that figure had been cut almost in half.[49]

Not all of Jencks's news is good. Many of the improvements in poor children's standard of living took place chiefly in the 1970s. More important, Jencks and Mayer's analysis assessed the status of children but did not address the poorest of the poor—the homeless—or the deteriorating economic prospects of poor single males, whose burgeoning numbers helped generate the homeless explosion of the 1980s. Some workers, especially young adults without high school diplomas, have plainly fared poorly over the last quarter century. In his 1994 book *The Homeless,* Jencks estimates that the number of Americans sleeping in shelters or public places roughly tripled between 1980 and 1990.[50]

Still, it is unlikely that most of the upsurge in homelessness resulted from an uneven economy, the liberals' leading villain behind the nation's purported decline. Even cities with low unemployment rates continue to have large homeless populations. A more likely culprit is the well-intentioned social policies that ultimately went awry from the late 1960s and 1970s. Deinstitutionalizing the mentally ill and cutting back on involuntary commitment were supposed to move the mentally ill from snake pit–like asylums to outpatient community facilities. The decriminalization of public drunkenness and the striking down of vagrancy laws were supposed to get drunks out of jails and into detoxification programs and aftercare treatment facilities. And the destruction of filthy skid-row flophouses was supposed to aid the cause of urban development and public safety. As a result of these policies, though, there was an overload of demand for the low-cost housing that Americans who were impoverished and dysfunctional had relied upon in earlier eras.

Other changes that boosted the ranks of the homeless, such as a decline in the real value of welfare benefits and the advent of crack cocaine, have less benign origins. But the cumulative impact of these shifts after 1973 contributed, eventually, to making hundreds of thousands of Americans homeless, at least for a time. In recent decades, most Americans have bettered their economic lot, but a small, desperately needy minority has not.

Pocketbook Voting and Economic Inequality

It is telling that most voters felt that the rich were getting richer and the poor were getting poorer *before* the upsurge in homelessness and income inequality. In 1995, 79 percent of Americans agreed with the statement that "the rich get richer and the poor get poorer." Yet an almost identical percentage of Americans (77 percent) felt that way in 1977, four years before Ronald Reagan took office and the so-called decade of greed commenced.[51]

Even though the electorate always seems to believe that inequality is rising, most workers tend to number themselves among the lucky few who have prospered. The 1994 elections marked the debut of the "angry" voter. But a Yankelovich poll taken a few weeks before the election found that less than 20 percent of the public thought their own family was doing poorly financially, and just 10 percent thought their family would be worse off two years down the road.[52] If Americans voted based on their pocketbooks, Democrats would have swept the 1994 election, instead of being routed.

Voters' bifurcated view of the economy—I'm doing well, others are faltering—continues to have profound consequences for presidential and congressional elections. Political scientists and lawmakers have claimed for years that the state of the econ-

omy powerfully influences voters. The adage of Clinton campaign adviser James Carville—"It's the economy, Stupid"—was
perhaps the most memorable maxim of the 1992 election. The
theory of sociotropic voting suggests that voters cast their ballots
based less on their own financial success—less on their own
pocketbook, if you will—than on how they think the nation is
faring economically, or how they think a candidate will influence the overall course of the economy in the years ahead. In
1994, most voters thought the economy was in a recession and
accordingly voted against the incumbents. Democratic pollster
Ruy Teixeira and political scientist Joel Rogers documented a
huge 25-point shift against the Democrats from 1992 among
voters who thought the economy was not so good or poor.[53]

The economy actually grew steadily throughout 1994,
though most voters at the time thought otherwise. By the 1996
election, a majority of Americans had finally concluded the
economy was expanding, and Clinton was reelected based on
the uptick in electoral optimism. The optimism gap may thus
help explain the lurching quality of elections in 1992, 1994, and
1996, where incumbents were unseated and ideological "revolu-
tions" seemed firmly in place—only to be undone in the next
election cycle. Carville's maxim perhaps needs to be modified. It
would be more accurate to state, "It's what voters *think* the
economy is, Stupid."

Slowing the Alarmism Cycle

More and more, as affluence spreads throughout humanity, our species' biggest problem will be a lack of satisfying challenges—opportunities to sacrifice, to make a large contribution to a larger cause, to be part of a team, to achieve nobility.

JULIAN SIMON[1]

For the foreseeable future, pop alarmism about the nation will likely continue. Americans seem doomed to follow the Reverse Cassandra rule, which holds that all cries of impending catastrophe must be heeded.[2]

In some instances, it is understandable why voters *feel* as though the country is in rapid decline. The average citizen may enjoy higher living standards today than 20 years ago, but economic advances since 1974 have come at a much slower pace than from 1945 to 1973. Through the perverse magic of what sociologists call "relative deprivation," the slowing of progress sometimes feels like an undoing of it; keeping up with the Joneses just gets harder and harder, as many dual-earner families can attest. Other trends may make an ongoing problem suddenly feel more menacing. While the homicide rate is down, more murder victims are killed by strangers today than in the past. Violent crime among juveniles also rose rapidly between 1988 and 1994,[3] feeding voters' conviction that they are more at risk today than ever before.

The Iron Triangle

Much of the time, however, public fears about America's future stem from a kind of iron triangle of alarmism created by the media, advocacy groups, and business lobbyists. Start with the press, the public's stealth filter of the external world, whose role is central since most voters acknowledge that they draw conclusions about conditions in America from what they see or read about in the media rather than from personal experience.

The imbalance between information garnered from the media and information garnered from personal experience is huge. A 1996 poll sponsored by the Kaiser Family Foundation and the *Washington Post* found that about 60 percent of the public said they got most of their news and information about national politics from television, while another 27 percent said they depended on newspapers or newsmagazines. Just 3 percent of those polled said they relied on family, friends, or coworkers.[4]

This dependence on the media alters the way people think about society. When members of the public are asked why they think the nation has a bad crime problem, three in four cite what they have seen on TV or read in the news. Only about a quarter of Americans base their beliefs about crime on personal experience.[5]

Voters, in short, often reach judgments about society by relying on hearsay evidence writ large. And as it turns out, the people who help make the news—advocates, business leaders, politicians, and reporters—all, for their own reasons, have a vested interest in acting like Chicken Littles.

Consider the case of the environment. Since the first Earth Day in 1970, scientists have amassed abundant evidence that the environment has, in many respects, become cleaner and safer. In his 1995 book *A Moment on the Earth,* journalist Gregg Easterbrook distills that evidence in lay terms.[6] He notes that since 1970, smog in the United States is down by a third, acid rain has been cut nearly in half, and twice as many rivers and lakes are now safe for swimming and fishing. Comedians have joked perennially about Los Angeles's smog, but the region has about 40 percent less smog today than in 1970, even though the number of cars in the area has tripled.[7] Nationally, the air is much cleaner. The Environmental Protection Agency's most recent annual report on national air quality and emissions found that all of the country's major air pollutants (except for nitrogen oxides) declined significantly from 1970 to 1995. This drop took place during a time when the U.S. population increased 28 percent and the mileage traveled by drivers more than doubled.[8]

Yet someone watching TV, or reading the daily newspaper, would likely feel disheartened about the state of the environment. The 1996 Kaiser Family Foundation poll found that 57 percent of Americans believed air quality was worse that year than 20 years earlier, and just 18 percent thought it was better.[9]

That misimpression stems partly from the fact that the people generating media coverage of the environment find hyperbole to be to their advantage. No protest movement can succeed for long without a villain. So it is not surprising that environmental advocacy groups' fund-raising hinges on the notion that the environment is in woeful shape and is either deteriorating or soon will be, without intervention. Few reporters receive press releases from environmental groups that begin with language such as "In yet another example of a remarkable success story, such-and-such pollution problem has markedly diminished. . . ."

Meanwhile, corporate America is too busy complaining about the toll environmental regulations take on business to champion the progress the nation is making. So reporters are unlikely to receive press releases from the National Association of Manufacturers that start with "In yet another example of successful regulatory intervention, the federal government has banned, at little cost, the production of ozone-destroying chemicals, including such and-such . . ." Finally, reporters themselves are generally uninterested in success stories. An old journalism adage holds that if there are 1,000 houses in a neighborhood and one burns down, the next day's story is about the house that burned, not the 999 that are marvels of safe construction.

The New Boob Tube Alarmism

Journalists have never shown much penchant for tales of success, but they have become even more cynical, and perhaps more alarmist, in recent decades. Like other news media, television presents a distorted picture of reality. In the 1990s, however, that picture grew even more contorted than in earlier decades. Network newscasts, for example, have become more beholden to the maxim "If it bleeds, it leads," even though violent crime has been dropping. According to the Center for Media and Public Affairs, the three network evening news shows broadcast 1,617 stories on domestic crime in 1997, more than the *combined* number of stories aired on the economy, business, the Clinton scandals, and military/defense issues. It's not just that crime has emerged as the top subject on the evening news. The fact is that the number of crime stories on the evening news has more than doubled since 1990. Even *after* excluding stories on the O. J. Simpson murder trial, the center's analysis found a 467 percent increase in the coverage of murders on the network evening news from 1992 to 1997, a period during which the actual number of homicides declined by about 25 percent.[10]

In February 1996, *U.S. News* asked the center to monitor all the ABC, CBS, and NBC morning, evening, and prime-time news shows for one week, along with the top-rated local evening newscast in Washington, D.C. The week's news was not especially dramatic; it was dominated by the Republican presidential primaries. But the newscasts still oozed alarmism. The center's study found that in 59.5 hours of coverage, the TV news operations ran 266 stories that by subject matter or on-air interpretation conveyed a sense of risk or peril—an average of 4.5 such stories per hour. Of the 42 stories during the week that mentioned trends in American life, 4 in 5 described negative or fearful trends, compared with 1 in 5 that described hopeful ones.[11] Robert Lichter, the center's director, said that when "you looked at the week, you saw violent crimes, disasters, accidents, wars, diseases, essentially an overwhelming portrayal of general misery. The overall picture was that America's in decline."[12]

Local television coverage is every bit as bad, if not worse. Hyped news from local stations is especially consequential because by 1996 the local evening newscast had supplanted the network news shows as Americans' single most important source of news.[13] Content analyses of local news coverage in 1997 show that stories about crime vastly outnumber every other subject—and account for more news stories than segments on economics, business, health, and government combined. The flip side of the preoccupation with crime is that local news routinely ignores important stories about other regional concerns. The Rocky Mountain Media Watch evaluation of 100 local newscasts aired one night in February 1997 found that only 2 percent of the coverage was devoted to environmental issues and just under 2 percent dealt with education.[14] That extreme imbalance has almost certainly skewed state spending and policies in the

1990s. If local television news devoted just 2 percent of its coverage to crime, it seems unlikely that corrections spending would be rising four or five times as fast as education spending in major media-market states, such as California and Pennsylvania.[15]

Other, less quantifiable shifts in journalism have also upped the cynicism and hysteria of media coverage in recent decades. In the post-Watergate era, one of the first lessons a young reporter learns on coming to Washington is that there is nothing worse than looking as if a government official snookered you into believing something that may not be true. With the proliferation of tabloid news productions like *Hard Copy,* and journalistic mud-wrestling forums, such as *The McLaughlin Group* and its spinoffs, television news has grown more rabid and less committed to educating viewers about public policy issues. Rush Limbaugh has supplanted Edward Murrow; Larry King has replaced Walter Cronkite.

Television plays an especially insidious role in fanning alarmism because viewers tend to think that seeing is believing. The 1997 Roper Starch Worldwide poll showed that if Americans received conflicting reports of the same news story from television and newspapers, they were more than twice as likely to believe the television report as the print story.[16]

Beyond its seeming creditability, television makes the atypical incident look far more commonplace than it really is and dims the memory of earlier hardships and atrocities. Few teenagers may still read Theodore Dreiser's *An American Tragedy* in school, and of those who do, even fewer know that Dreiser's novel was based on the real-life story of a notorious cad named Chester Gillette, who drowned his pregnant girlfriend in 1906 so he could pursue another woman. In an infamous case in 1994, Susan Smith, a woman from a small town in South Carolina, bundled her children into a car and drowned them in a lake, too. Law enforcement officials suggested she murdered her children to please a man with whom she allegedly had a brief affair but who did not want kids.[17]

The Smith murders prompted Newt Gingrich to decry the "sickness of our society."[18] But Smith's horrifying act said less about a newfound sickness in American society than about the capacity of television news to amplify the visibility of sick acts. It is hard to imagine that thirty years ago a Susan Smith would have gone on television to issue a phony appeal to find her children's abductor and have her story telecast nationwide, hour to hour.

Media coverage might actually narrow the optimism gap if viewers thought it overstated the seriousness of social problems. They don't. The nightmare of every public relations executive, one grounded in experience, is that while consumers readily believe bad news, they are not inclined to accept good news. After the 1996 election, Louis Harris and Associates questioned some 3,000 Americans about their views on the news media. Just 2 percent said the media were "too positive," and 61 percent said the media were too negative. But most members of the public didn't think the media exaggerated the seriousness of problems with its drumbeat of bad news. Just over 60 percent of those polled said that the news media either reported the scope of problems accurately or minimized them.[19]

One might think that all of the bad news on television would eventually make Americans feel personally threatened, too. But television viewing turns out to largely reinforce the line Americans draw between their own lives and other people's. Social scientists have discovered that the mass media have a "third person effect"—meaning that the viewer concludes media exposure has a large impact on *other* viewers but not on themselves. For instance, a national survey taken at the start of the decade found that 61 percent of Americans felt other consumers were more negatively influenced by X-rated material than themselves.[20]

Similarly, Americans who watch frequent television reports on crime "come to believe in the 'mean' world," write researchers Linda Heath and John Petraitis, yet "most of them do not live in it. . . . Frequent viewers tend to see their own worlds as havens in the midst of the violence 'out there.' "[21] Professor Al Gunther of the University of Wisconsin at Madison and his colleague Paul Mundy wryly sum up the mass media's impact by noting that Americans often express the sentiment "most people believe anything they see in print"—but that most citizens then quickly insist that the label "most people" doesn't apply to them.[22] Or, as Fathali Moghaddam, a psychology professor at Georgetown University, puts it, "The sky is falling, but not on me."[23]

Shrinking the Optimism Gap

Narrowing the optimism gap requires cultural change or a shift in attitudes more than it requires policy or legislative reforms. It is likely to resist any hard-and-fast solution. Revising people's sense of expectation is especially difficult in a society and time that lack an overwhelming national crisis and sense of necessity. But the general direction of steps that would help seems clear. The organizing principle for dealing with the optimism gap ought to be that members of the public, the press, politicians, and advocates strive to narrow Americans' sense of distance and separateness from "others." There are many ways to pursue this end, short of fabricating a crisis or urging people to join hands and sing "Kumbaya." Conversely, initiatives that remind Americans of the pleasures, fears, and doubts that they collectively share might restore a greater sense of common purpose.

What Advocates Can Do

A good place to begin is with the overheated rhetoric of advocates. In some instances, activists' rhetoric literally promotes distrust of strangers. John Walsh became an advocate for missing children after the abduction and gruesome murder of his six-year-old son, Adam, in 1981. But when Walsh testified before Congress in the early 1980s that 50,000 kids were kidnapped by strangers each year, he spawned a huge industry of fear, from the millions of milk cartons of "missing kids" to the parents who tagged their children with electronic homing devices. Virtually all of these abductions were in fact noncustodial parents who nabbed their kids from alienated ex-spouses, and the missing-kid scare has now receded.[24] Even when advocates are not explicitly warning people off of strangers, however, they routinely promote a picture of the world as overwhelmed with woe and fearsome threats.

Suggesting that professional advocates moderate their alarmism sounds naive, since alarmism is typically part of an advocate's modus operandi. Yet the activists' assumption that no harm can come from exaggerating the various menaces facing the country also displays a kind of naïveté and shortsightedness.

In his 1968 best-seller *The Population Bomb,* Paul Ehrlich opened with this declaration: "The battle to feed all of humanity is over. In the 1970s, the world will undergo famines— hundreds of millions of people are going to starve to death in spite of any crash programs embarked upon now."[25] The following year Ehrlich duly predicted that before 1980 the world's oceans would be dead, and the Japanese and Chinese would be starving for lack of fish and other seafood in their diet.[26] By 1975, Ehrlich had announced that "the world is teetering on the brink of mass starvation."[27]

Ehrlich, of course, was wrong in all of these horrifying predictions. But how did he justify his hyperbole? As far back as *The Population Bomb,* Ehrlich acknowledged that "any scientist lives constantly with the possibility that he may be wrong." But he argued that even if his projections of an impending population explosion were "wrong, people will still be better fed, better housed and happier" as a result.[28] The reason people would be better off, in Ehrlich's view, is that scaring voters prompts them to act. "Everyone wants to know what's going to happen. And you never know what's going to happen," Ehrlich explained to *Stanford* magazine in 1990. "So, the question is, Do you say 'I don't know,' in which case they all go back to bed—or do you say, 'Hell, in ten years you're likely to be going without food and water' and [get] their attention?"[29]

People are sheep, in other words, and they need to be awakened to the wolf who lurks nearby. Yet neither Ehrlich nor the many doomsayers who have followed the same logic seem to worry that exaggerated predictions about pending calamities may immobilize people instead of galvanizing them. Like crying wolf too many times, false alarms can elevate people's skepticism rather than spurring them to change their ways. To cite the most poignant example, the issue of overpopulation, which prompted Ehrlich's best-seller, largely disappeared from public debate not long after his overwrought predictions failed to materialize. Today, the problem of overpopulation continues to plague some regions of the world, but most Americans don't give any thought to the problem.[30]

On one domestic issue after another the pattern is similar: The apocalypse-now rhetoric of advocates numbs voters and skews social policy. For much of the 1980s, reporters and government officials duly recited as fact the claim made by Mitch Snyder and other homeless advocates that 3 million Americans were homeless each night. The 3 million number turned out to be little more than a back-of-the-envelope calculation. Researchers subsequently discovered that the actual number was one-fifth that.

When lawmakers belatedly started raising questions about Snyder's 3 million estimate, he dismissed the "gnawing curiosity" for more precise numbers as the work of "Western little minds." Still, even a Zen master can see that the homeless problem is far more manageable if it is five times smaller than previously advertised.[31] When a social problem seems too overwhelming, people may blame "the system" or end up feeling powerless. Eventually, the overheated rhetoric of Snyder and other homeless advocates helped dampen public interest in attacking the homeless problem. By the end of the decade, despairing activists had already started complaining that the taxpayer was developing "compassion fatigue."

Soon, another seemingly insuperable social ill—the crack baby plague—appeared. It, too, was vastly exaggerated. When the National Association for Perinatal Addiction Research and Education reported that 375,000 babies were born annually who had been exposed to drugs in the womb, Congress held hearings, newsmagazines ran cover stories, and before long it seemed clear the country was confronting an epidemic of irremediably ruined crack babies in need of foster care and adoptive parents.[32] In fact, the 375,000 figure was the number of mothers who drank or took a drug at any point in their pregnancy. The real number of crack-addicted infants was closer to 35,000, and many of these children later shook off the more crippling effects of their dependency.[33]

It is no small irony that when advocates play Chicken Little for "a good cause," or engage in "lying for justice," they often perversely influence government programs to redirect resources *away* from the social ill the activists want solved. Writing in the *Washington Monthly* in 1997, Glenn Hodges summarized how the advocates' rhetoric had fouled up government efforts to aid rape victims and those at risk for AIDS:

> Transforming debatable studies into steadfast slogans—one in three [women] will be victimized [by rape]—universalizes the problem: All women are equally vulnerable. But it's poor and minority women who are at the highest risk, and middle-class

white women—especially college students—who get most of the support services. According to the U.S. Department of Justice's National Crime Survey, black women are more than twice as likely to be raped as white women, and low-income women are raped five times as often as high-income women. Meanwhile, as community rape crisis centers are habitually underfunded and short-staffed, their well-funded university counterparts in some instances may have little reason for being: Many universities— even large state schools—report fewer than one rape or at-tempted rape each year. . . . Instead of "taking back the night" on college campuses, energies might be better spent volunteering at local rape crisis centers.[34]

Government spending on AIDS has been similarly mistar-geted—thanks in part to the efforts of AIDS activists and fed-eral officials to portray the virus as a threat to the heterosexual community, rather than as a disease that overwhelmingly afflicts gay men and IV drug users. Hodges again:

> The most devastating consequence of the CDC's [U.S. Centers for Disease Control] errant public information campaign has been the misdirection of AIDS prevention money. In California, only 9 percent of the state's AIDS prevention funds targeted gay men between 1989 and 1992, despite the fact that they repre-sented 85 percent of all AIDS cases. . . . Twenty percent of the CDC's $584 million AIDS prevention budget goes toward HIV testing. But of the 2.4 million federally funded tests given in 1994, only 13 percent were for gay or bisexual men or IV drug users.[35]

Activists could constrain Americans' optimism gap if they analyzed social ills in less catastrophic terms. Gresham's law— bad money drives out good—is equally applicable to the subject of public dangers. To paraphrase Gresham, false alarms drive out true ones.

What the Press and Politicians Can Do

Journalists, too, can help narrow the optimism gap, by gaining a greater command of history and becoming more adept at sorting through statistics. History is the enemy of exaggeration. It is hard to write, say, that it is tougher than ever to be a mother if one knows something about the grueling lives of mothers 100 years ago.[36] Similarly, a TV journalist who knows the history of the depression would have difficulty standing outside a shuttered auto plant and proclaiming that American workers now feel unprecedented fears about their job security.

Today's reporters are generally better versed in economics, history, and statistics than earlier generations of journalists. The working press today has many talented journalists who dissect government statistics and distill academic research. Yet while press coverage is now better informed, there is still plenty of opportunity for improvement, particularly on television. A study by Professor Ted Smith of almost 14,000 economics stories broadcast by the network news between 1982 and 1987 found that on-air reporters were unrelentingly downbeat, even when the economy was booming. From 1984 to 1987, one of the more robust economic periods in the century, only about 5 percent of the stories portrayed the economy in a positive light.[37]

If history is the enemy of exaggeration, it can also be the enemy of editors and news producers. When a reporter is writing or filming a story on deadline about ghetto poverty, he or she is not likely to ask the editor for extra time to thumb through Jacob Riis's 1890 classic, *How the Other Half Lives.* Narrowing the optimism gap, in short, would require members of the media to work at odds with their institutional imperatives to get pieces done "fast and dirty"—just as advocates' toning down their alarmism would cut across the grain of their institutional traditions and fund-raising efforts.

For their part, politicians could help shrink the optimism gap by moderating their time-honored instincts to discover new crises and then exaggerate their own capacity to solve them. When every social ill constitutes a "crisis," the term starts to lose its meaning. Journalist Nicholas Lemann cites the example of Newt Gingrich's oft-repeated claim in his speeches that "no civilization can survive with 12-year-olds having babies, with 15-year-olds killing each other, with 17-year-olds dying of AIDS, with 18-year-olds getting diplomas they can't read."[38] When Gingrich reels off this chronology of this loss of national innocence, audiences clap and nod in knowing appreciation. But as Lemann points out, Gingrich's recital is misleading and incapacitating:

> How many 12-year-olds, really, are having babies? When there actually is a crisis, what will there be left to say that will rouse the nation, and not be discounted by a public that has been hearing inflated talk for years? When politicians use the easy, dramatic language of social crisis, it has a strange, disabling effect on the government. The biggest language guns are being hauled out, the deepest and most intimate connection to public forged, with regard to a problem that government can't do much about. . . . The more central that government officials make social disarray appear to be, the less central government becomes as a problem-solving institution in the society.[39]

Presidents and legislators often make more campaign promises than they can fulfill, but their promises started getting ever more grandiose—and thus inevitably disappointing—in the 1960s. Overpromising began to exacerbate voter distrust of the government, and it bolstered taxpayers' belief that the government routinely wastes vast sums of money trying to fix intractable social problems. Put another way, overpromising made the outside world look worse than it really was. By setting the bar for success too high, lawmakers made even successful programs look like duds. When he sponsored the Clean Air Act, Senator Edmund Muskie declared it would ensure "that all Americans in all parts of the country shall have clean air to breathe" in just a few years. It took more than a few years, but the air Americans breathe is notably cleaner than in Muskie's day. Yet the air today is hardly pristine. "Only against that absolutist standard can our efforts to control air pollution be judged a failure," writes columnist Jacob Weisberg.[40]

Just like the advocates, politicians defend themselves by arguing that lofty goals are all for a good cause. When Jimmy Carter set up the Atlanta Project in the early 1990s to empower residents of inner-city Atlanta's poorest neighborhoods, he was motivated by "the lack of awareness in the Atlanta hierarchy . . . of the plight of poverty-stricken people . . . something needed to be done."[41] At the Atlanta Project's founding, Carter announced, "I would like to set an optimum goal in every area: housing, unemployment, school dropouts, drug addiction and so forth, the maximum achievable goal that would be at all practical."[42]

Five years later, the project had sponsored lots of meetings and consultations with local residents and had generated some useful initiatives that provided childhood immunizations and a modest number of jobs. But the Atlanta Project had little discernible impact on poverty, housing, unemployment, school dropouts, and drug addiction.[43] Carter complained that critics were measuring the Atlanta Project against "a standard of perfection—a standard of totally eradicating poverty from the city of Atlanta in four years, which is obviously ridiculous." But he also confessed, "I was the one responsible for raising the expectations too high."[44] In 1996, the staff, scope, and budget of the Atlanta Project were all sharply scaled back.

The cumulative effect of several decades of overpromising is such that most voters now doubt whether the federal government can accomplish much of anything. In January 1997, most

Americans anticipated that Clinton and congressional Republicans would not make progress toward balancing the budget during Clinton's second term, and that most of the problems with both Medicare and Social Security funding would not be resolved in the second term.[45] People's low expectations for the federal government swept across other policy areas as well, according to a *New York Times*/CBS News poll taken around the time of the inaugural. Only one in three members of the public thought the nation's education system would be better by the end of Clinton's second term, and just 18 percent believed fewer people would be living in poverty.[46]

To bolster faith in government, it is not enough that most people have good experiences with bureaucrats; fewer people must also have bad experiences. As political scientists learned a quarter century ago, positive personal experiences with government agencies do not boost people's overall trust of government, but bad experiences further weaken it.[47] Most politicians and members of the press tend to pay little attention to management reforms to curb waste and make government agencies more accountable because they lack the glamor and drama of elections and major policy pronouncements. Nonetheless, efforts to simply make government workers more helpful and courteous might go surprisingly far toward restoring people's faith in civil servants and public institutions.

What the Public Can Do

Voters, too, can play a part in reducing the optimism gap. As journalist Mickey Kaus has noted, widespread income inequalities seem destined to remain a part of American society, an inevitable reflection of people's differing talents, opportunities, and drive. But *social inequality*—the gap in the public sphere between the rich, the middle class, and the poor—can be narrowed. In *The End of Equality,* Kaus urges voters and lawmakers to adopt a program of "civic liberalism" that would constrain or eliminate differences in the way government institutions treat citizens. The jury system and the ballot box, for example, foster social equality because everyone is eligible to serve, and everyone's vote, no matter what his or her income, has equal weight.[48]

Public parks, well-run mass transit systems, libraries, and museums are other institutions that help sustain social equality. The corporate world has its equivalents. Companies, for example, that encourage or require employees to periodically switch jobs or to produce products with teams of coworkers typically have a more egalitarian ethos. Some savvy corporations even use diversity training to remind their multiethnic workforces of their common goals, as opposed to simply underscoring workers' unique interests.[49]

In short, civic liberalism could shrink the optimism gap by closing the social distance Americans now feel from each other. Among other reforms, Kaus recommends that lawmakers enact a mandatory national service program for older teens (either military or civilian service), that the government eliminate the welfare system and substitute a program of guaranteed low-wage public service jobs available to any American who wants to work, and that Congress enact a national health care system.[50]

All of these reforms would buttress people's sense of social equality. Americans would no longer stigmatize welfare recipients as lazy or undeserving once they toiled at jobs. Graduates of elite prep schools would work side by side with high school dropouts to fulfill their national service requirement, and rich and poor patients alike would share the same waiting rooms outside doctors' offices. At present, none of these proposals has a chance of being enacted by Congress. As Kaus acknowledges, they also are expensive and sure to produce embarrassing boondoggles. Yet despite all its inefficiencies, civic liberalism provides a kind of guidepost for restoring a sense of shared purpose. And it's worth remembering that it wasn't all that long ago that the draft did impose a common obligation on young men of various social classes.

Cultural shifts that might reduce the optimism gap are perhaps harder to sketch than changes in public policy. As a general rule, changes to the zeitgeist that made Americans less mistrustful would also curb the I'm OK–They're Not syndrome. Voters who trust other individuals are much more likely to have confidence in the Congress, the president, and the courts than voters who distrust other individuals. They also are less likely to believe that government action hurts people.[51]

As the Internet expands, it could refurbish Americans' sense of trust. At the very least, the Internet empowers users to escape their dependence on television for information about other communities. Unlike television, which usually paints a frightening picture of distant places, the Internet allows people to interact and to hear firsthand from other individuals about commonly shared concerns, joys, and doubts. Professor Sherry Turkle of the Massachusetts Institute of Technology believes that "when people join some kind of Internet community—and not just chat rooms—but a real international community, it makes distant things seem a lot closer. It lessens people's split vision of the world."[52] Other experts are less sanguine. They worry that the vast array of chat groups and bulletin boards on the Internet might simply add to people's sense of balkanization or paranoia, in part because the Internet can spread nutty rumors rapidly.

The last—and perhaps most elusive—way to narrow the optimism gap is to reduce people's expectations. Even modestly deflating taxpayers' sense of personal entitlement would help. In the past, more workers accepted the fact that their wages might stagnate or rise slowly than do so today. Life may not always maintain a steady arc of upward improvement, though it does much of the time. At the same time, voters could modestly raise, or at least modulate, their expectations of government and other institutions.

Taxpayers tend to harbor excessive expectations of what social programs should accomplish, while simultaneously lacking faith in the government's capacity to run effective programs. Voters would be more optimistic if they asked less of social programs. Once the rhetoric of overpromising was scaled back, the reputation of government agencies might improve, as the work of thousands of competent civil servants became more evident.

Many Americans, for example, believe that a successful welfare-to-work program should painlessly cut the public assistance rolls by a half or more.[53] That standard is out of reach for most state social service agencies. It is plausible, however, to expect that a top-notch jobs program might reduce the relief rolls by, say, 10 to 15 percent—and that the government could manage such a program without wasting taxpayer dollars. Lyndon Johnson was wrong when he contended the federal government would end poverty. But claims that the government cannot help the poor (or that efforts to do so can only make for more poverty) are just as exaggerated.

In the end, the private lives of Americans are probably not as happy as they claim, but neither is the society at large as dangerous as most Americans think. People's profound pessimism about the outside world, which seems to become more ingrained with each decade, is unhealthy in the long run. As Samuel Johnson once warned, "He that overvalues himself will undervalue others, and he that undervalues others will oppress them."[54]

In bygone eras, voters with optimistic outlooks could bear sacrifices and privations because they believed the future held great things for them and their children. By contrast, the cynicism of today's voters tends to undermine the legitimacy of doing things for the commonweal. It also provides a breeding ground for the paranoia and anger that in extreme cases erupts in terrorist acts, like the 1995 Oklahoma City bombing or the antigovernment and antitechnology screeds of the Unabomber.

Thomas Jefferson was fond of quoting the biblical proverb "Where there is no vision, the people perish." Perhaps Jefferson exaggerated. Yet his view of the importance of public purpose is a reminder that the present hostility toward government is not America's only political tradition. Today, it is hard to imagine a Rosie the Riveter leaving home to toil in a 1990s version of World War II factories in order to buttress the nation. That shared sense of vision will flourish again when more citizens perceive "them" to be much like "us."

Good, the more communicated,
the more abundant grows.

JOHN MILTON[1]

Not long after I started work on *The Optimism Gap* in 1995, I sent an early draft of several chapters to William Whitworth, the editor of the *Atlantic Monthly.* Having some years earlier written a piece for Whitworth, I asked him if he was interested in publishing the story as an *Atlantic Monthly* cover piece. Submitting the piece showed some chutzpah, since I expressly criticized the *Atlantic* for the alarmist tone it had taken on the subject of crime.[2] A few weeks later, Whitworth sent me a gracious note declining to publish the article. "I confess that for me it invites argument at every turn," he wrote.[3]

Inviting argument at every turn can be a good thing, if the provocation makes people reexamine their prejudices. A contrarian book like *The Optimism Gap* is bound to invite such argument.

In arguing the case for American progress in the last quarter century, I want to be clear that I am not claiming that the era of Pangloss, Voltaire's foolishly optimistic doctor, has arrived. The nation's social ills have not vanished, and in many cases they remain acute. In the last quarter century, novel maladies like AIDS have appeared. At the same time, policymakers have learned much more about problems that may have been building for decades, such as global warming. In the decade to come, fearsome new social problems could well erupt again. "It is legitimate to deplore certain trends and developments in any society as malign or destructive," writes the historian Arthur Herman. "It is quite another thing to draw, or allow to be drawn, a picture that suggests that these problems have such deeply rooted causes that they are unsolvable, or have such far-reaching implications that only a drastic overhaul of the society or culture as a whole can fix them."[4]

To Herman's point, I would add one other. As a rule, even after new problems arise, most Americans are still better off than in the past. Typically, new social and environmental ills are less serious problems than those of the past. AIDS is a horrible epidemic, as anyone can attest who has lost a family member, friend, or lover to it. Yet even after the arrival of this deadly plague, most Americans live longer and have more healthy days than before. New problems, of course, can also spawn novel solutions, such as the inventions of new life-prolonging drugs for treating HIV. Thanks in part to the new drugs, the death rate from AIDS fell 26 percent in the United States in 1996, the first such decline since the onset of the epidemic.[5]

As the nation continues to advance, critics can be counted on to lament the hidden costs of progress. With the history of earlier declinists as a guide, the skeptics will surely claim that Americans' current material abundance is really a secret curse that twists people's values and undermines traditional ties to family and community. Yet the longing for a "simpler time" usually does not run deep. The vast majority of Americans seem to think all the opportunities and "things" that they lacked in the past—the VCRs, the second cars, the cellular phones, the color televisions, the overseas travel, the postgrad education, and the newfound leisure time—add to their sense of happiness, not just to their credit card bills and material cravings. People may not say that the abundance of consumer products and services is a sign of progress, yet they act as if it was. That is why the queue of people who genuinely wish to pass their lives without conveniences and luxuries is short. "Trading places" is a popular concept in the movies. But few Americans would really choose to live in a less affluent time.[6]

With the close of the millennium upon us shortly, it is inevitable that signs proclaiming "The End Is Near" will proliferate. Americans can counter this looming onslaught of fin de siècle pessimism by doing something that now seems almost un-American: have faith in good news.[7]

In 1997, a majority of the public finally concluded that the economy was performing reasonably well. And there is even a kind of triumphalism at present in some corners of the press about how the world should take lessons from the U.S. economy. Yet this uptick in optimism came only after the economy had enjoyed seven years of growth, inflation fell to its lowest level in 30 years, unemployment dropped to its lowest level in peacetime since 1957, the Dow rocketed to record levels, real family incomes rose, and the economies of our Asian competitors faltered.[8]

Even this cautious public economic optimism barely budged people's underlying pessimism about the direction of the country or restored their faith in the future. In 1997, polls typically showed that less than half the public thought the nation was moving in the "right direction," and most Americans still believed the current generation of kids would fare worse than their parents.[9] Then, finally, in the first half of 1998, the mood became somewhat more upbeat: A slight majority of Americans concluded that the nation was moving in the right direction. Ironically, however, this newfound optimism appeared to stem from the troubling news in January 1998 that

Bill Clinton had sought to conceal what was then considered an alleged sexual affair with White House intern Monica Lewinsky.

The truth is that only days before the Lewinsky saga broke, polls showed that most people still did not think that the country was moving in the right direction or feel satisfied with the way things were going in the nation.[10] A few days later, amid all the loose talk-show chatter about impeachment, roughly 60 percent of the electorate decided that the nation was moving in the right direction after all. As Richard Morin of the *Washington Post* put it, "By focusing a harsh spotlight on the Oval Office, the scandal may have inadvertently opened America's eyes to just how well-off we are as a nation."[11] It is telling as well, if not altogether surprising, that so many Americans responded to the Clinton sex scandals through the prism of the I'm OK– They're Not syndrome. Most people, that is, claimed that they themselves had no interest in the news stories on President Clinton's sex life—though they were convinced that other people were interested or even fascinated by the coverage.[12]

William Bennett may have best summed up the zeitgeist of the day when he observed that "these are times in which conservatives are going to have to face the fact that there is some good news on the landscape. We're going to have to learn to live with it."[13] In some measure, Bennett's curmudgeonly response to good news reflects the fact that conservatives are loath to credit Bill Clinton for progress. But his begrudging acceptance of the good news is also part of an age-old tradition. From era to era, the electorate's mood has swung from boosterish optimism—as during the first two decades after World War II—to the stubborn skepticism popular today. Over a century ago, Charles Dickens deftly captured this skeptical attitude toward politics and public life in his travel journal, *American Notes*. "It is an essential part of every national character to pique itself mightily upon its faults," he observed, "and to deduce tokens of its virtue or its wisdom from their very exaggeration." In America's case, Dickens argued, the "one great blemish in the popular mind . . . and the prolific parent of an innumerable brood of evils, is Universal Distrust. Yet the American citizen plumes himself upon this spirit, even when he is sufficiently dispassionate to perceive the ruin it works; and will often adduce it . . . as an instance of the great sagacity and acuteness of the people."[14]

Americans today continue to plume themselves on their skepticism. Violent crime has plummeted. But the 1997 Harris poll shows that 2 in 3 adults think crime is on the rise, with almost half saying it is increasing "a lot."[15] The AIDS death rate is down. Yet less than a third of the public thinks so.[16] The budget deficit has almost been eliminated. Yet the *Wall Street Journal* reports that its year-end 1997 survey of over 2,000 Americans found that more people believe in Santa Claus than believe the federal budget will be balanced in five years.[17] As the millennium draws to an end, voters might resolve to take a bit less pride in the distrust that Dickens lamented so long ago. I believe that Americans can take heart from the good news without becoming a nation of self-satisfied Pollyannas.

NOTES

FOREWORD

1. When social scientists compared children whose mothers worked to children from apparently similar families whose mothers did not work, they found few consistent differences. See Lois Wladis Hoffman, "Effects of Maternal Employment in the Two-Parent Family," *American Psychologist,* vol. 44 (February 1989), 283–92 and the sources cited there.

2. George Akerlof, Janet Yellen, and Michael Katz, "Analysis of Out-of-Wedlock Childbearing in the United States," *Quarterly Journal of Economics,* vol. 111 (May 1996), 277–317.

INTRODUCTION

1. To the best of my knowledge, Andrew Kohut coined the term "the optimism gap." Kohut is director of the Pew Research Center for the People & the Press in Washington, D.C. See Pew Research Center for the People & the Press, "The Optimism Gap Grows," news release, January 17, 1997; and Charles Madigan, "The Optimism Gap," *Chicago Tribune,* March 4, 1997.

2. Frank I. Luntz, "Americans Talk About the American Dream," in Lamar Alexander and Chester E. Finn, Jr., eds., *The New Promise of American Life* (Indianapolis, Ind.: Hudson Institute, 1995), 47.

3. Ibid., 54.

4. David W. Moore and Frank Newport, "People in the World Mostly Satisfied with Their Personal Lives," Gallup News Service, June 20, 1995, 5, tables 5 and 6.

5. Ibid., 2, 6–7.

6. Cited in Donald W. White, *The American Century: The Rise and Decline of the United States as a World Power* (New Haven and London: Yale University Press, 1996), 276.

7. See James Davison Hunter and Carl Bowman, *The State of Disunion: 1996 Survey of American Political Culture,* vol. 2, the Post-Modernity Project, University of Virginia (In Medias Res Educational Foundation, Ivy, Va.), 1996, summary tables 4.A through 4.Q.

A December 1997 survey of 1,009 adults by Opinion Research Corporation of Princeton, N.J., for the Gannett News Service suggested that Americans were slightly more sanguine in 1997 than in 1996 as to whether the nation was declining or advancing. It showed a plurality of Americans (46 percent) felt "America is on the decline," while 44 percent felt the country was "on the rise," Chuck Raasch, "Poll on How America's Doing Finds Rampant Ambiguity," *Idaho Statesman,* December 25, 1997.

8. Oscar Wilde, "Lady Windermere's Fan," in *The Complete Works of Oscar Wilde* (New York: Barnes & Noble Books, 1994), 417. George Bernard Shaw got at much the same thought when he wrote: "There are two tragedies in life. One is to lose your heart's desire. The other is to gain it." *Man and Superman* (London: Constable, 1952 ed.), 165.

9. Cited in Julian L. Simon, ed., *The State of Humanity* (Oxford, England, and Cambridge, Mass.: Blackwell, 1995), 6.

10. Lamar Alexander, *We Know What to Do* (New York: William Morrow, 1996), xi.

11. Cornel West, *Race Matters* (New York: Vintage Books, 1994), 9. Lest the reader think I have exaggerated West's declinist tone, he also asserts that "we are living in one of the most frightening moments in the history of this country" and that "the young black generation are up against forces of death, destruction, and disease unprecedented in the everyday life of black urban people" (155, 149).

12. Cited in Arthur Herman, *The Idea of Decline in Western History* (New York: Free Press, 1997), 2.

13. Transcript of President Clinton's Weekly Radio Address, White House Press Office, Washington, D.C., September 28, 1996 (reprinted on U.S. Newswire, September 30, 1996).

Not long ago, Senator Paul Wellstone managed to transmogrify the United States, in the space of two paragraphs, from a prosperous nation to one in danger of abandoning its moral principles. In a May 14, 1997, speech to the National Press Club in Washington, D.C., Wellstone said of our "quiet" crisis: "Our nation is now in its third century. To get here, we're survived the gravest of crises—war and depression, foreign dangers and domestic turbulence. . . . Now, in 1997, we face yet another crisis—not a war, not a broad economic calamity, but a crisis nonetheless. This is, by the averages and indicators, a prosperous time for our country, a time of sustained growth and low inflation, of a booming stock market and low unemployment. There's no blare of bugles, no moans of universal distress, no loud hordes of righteous protesters clamoring in our streets. But averages are misleading. They tell nothing of the ends of the curve, the height at the top or the depth at the bottom. And that's where our crisis resides, a quiet crisis, a crisis of money, power and injustice, a crisis of a nation in danger of abandoning the principles of equality and justice, that are so fundamental to our resilience, that are indeed the very meaning and purpose of America." Quoted in the "Culture, et Cetera" column of the *Washington Times,* May 21, 1997.

14. Richard Gephardt's remarks to the Children's Defense Fund, March 14, 1997, Webwire-Remarks, Congressional Press Releases, Federal Document Clearing House.

15. See John Mueller, "The Catastrophe Quota: Trouble After the Cold War," *Journal of Conflict Resolution,* vol. 38, no. 3 (September 1994), 355–75. Mueller writes that "to inspire or justify worry in the wake of the Cold War, trouble

spotters have ingeniously changed the meanings of several key words. One of these is *stability*. During the Cold War, instability was characteristically equated with the dangers of a nuclear war between the United States and the Soviet Union. It may not be completely irrelevant to recall in this regard that there was a time a few years ago when very many people were consumed by the concern that such a war might break out. Remember the sword of Damocles? . . . Remember the ticking doomsday clock on the cover of the *Bulletin of the Atomic Scientists?* . . . Other words with new definitions are *major war* and *global conflict*. Before 1989, major wars or global conflicts were conflagrations in which the big countries became viscerally and directly involved: the kind of thing that happened in World Wars I and II. However, former President Jimmy Carter made a speech about foreign policy at the 1992 Democratic National Convention . . . in which he announced that there were 35 'major wars' going on in the world. As he explained it later, he designated a major war as any conflict in which at least 1,000 people had been killed" (364–65).

16. Ibid., 357.

17. Derek Bok, *The State of the Nation* (Cambridge, Mass: Harvard University Press, 1996); Simon, *The State of Humanity;* Reynolds Farley, *The New American Reality* (New York: Russell Sage Foundation, 1996); Robert J. Samuelson, *The Good Life and Its Discontents: The American Dream in the Age of Entitlement, 1945–1995* (New York: Times Books, 1995). For the most part, Seymour Martin Lipset is also sanguine about progress in the United States in *American Exceptionalism: A Double-Edged Sword* (New York: Norton, 1996).

Two thoughtful, if less quantitative, books on American progress are journalist Michael Elliot's *The Day Before Yesterday* (New York: Simon & Schuster, 1996) and Bard college president Leon Botstein's *Jefferson's Children* (New York: Doubleday, 1997).

18. Derek Bok argues that international comparisons are pertinent to people and shows that the United States has not made social and economic progress as rapidly as six other industrial democracies since 1960. See Bok, *The State of the Nation,* 366–75, 392–404.

19. Aaron Wildavsky, "Doing Better and Feeling Worse: The Political Pathology of Health Policy," in John H. Knowles, ed., *Doing Better and Feeling Worse: Health in the United States* (New York: Norton, 1977), 106.

20. Arthur M. Schlesinger, Jr., *The Disuniting of America* (Knoxville, Tenn.: Whittle Direct Books, 1991), 62–63.

CHAPTER ONE: The New Pandora's Box

1. Cited in David G. Myers, *Social Psychology,* 2nd ed. (New York: McGraw-Hill, 1987), 89.

2. For data on Americans' convictions that they are better-than-average drivers, see O. Svenson, "Are We All Less Risky and More Skillful than Our Fellow Drivers?" *Acta Psychologica,* vol. 46 (1981), 143–48. An August 1997 *New York Times*/CBS News poll of 1,307 adults found that more than 9 out of 10 Americans rated themselves as good or excellent drivers, 7 percent said their driving skills were fair, and less than 1 percent said they had poor driving skills. By a

six-to-one margin, Americans thought drivers were less safe in 1997 than 10 years earlier—though if they themselves were in an accident, 47 percent said their car would be safer than average. Just 6 percent felt their car would be less safe than the average vehicle.

On people's belief that their jobs and home life compare favorably to those of other families, see Michaels Opinion Research, "American Family Values: Seventh National Survey," New York, October 1995 (sponsored by the Massachusetts Mutual Life Insurance Company), 4, 13, 29; Michaels Opinion Research, "National Public Opinion Survey: Commitment and American Society," New York, November 1994, MassMutual American Family Values Program, 6, 12, 24, 26, and the data tables in the appendixes; "Survey Reveals American Attitudes on the State of the Family," Church of Jesus Christ of Latter-Day Saints, news release, December 17, 1996, and the volume of cross-tabulations from the Gallup Organization, 56, 76, 87, 100, 112, 120, 144, 200; Wirthlin Worldwide, "Florida Statewide Benchmark Survey on Marriage," McLean, Va., October 1997 (prepared for the Florida Family Council), 1, 3, 4, 13, and 29.

On people's belief that they receive superior medical care, see Princeton Survey Research Associates, *The Kaiser/Harvard National Survey of Americans' Views on Managed Care,* Princeton, N.J., August 22 and September 23, 1997 (conducted for the Henry J. Kaiser Family Foundation and Harvard University); Lawrence R. Jacobs and Robert Y. Shapiro, "The Conventional Wisdom That Portrays Americans as Narrow Individualists Is Myopic," *Public Perspective,* May/June 1993, 23; Robert J. Blendon, "The Public's View of the Future of Health Care," *JAMA,* vol. 259, no. 24 (June 24, 1988), 3587.

Americans' convictions that their local public school is better than most other schools is well documented in the annual Phi Delta Kappa/Gallup polls of public attitudes toward public schools. See Stanley M. Elam et al., "The 28th Annual Phi Delta Kappa/Gallup Poll of the Public's Attitudes Toward the Public Schools," *Phi Delta Kappan,* vol. 78, no. 1 (September 1996), 41–60, and Elam, *How America Views Its Schools* (Bloomington, Ind.: Phi Delta Kappa Educational Foundation, 1995), 9–16. A chart illustrating the consistently different grades that Americans have awarded to schools at the local and national levels in the Phi Delta/Kappa polls from 1974 and 1995 is reproduced in "But Look at the Marks We give the Public Schools! Those Close to Home Look Better . . . but Not Good," *Public Perspective,* October/November 1995, 28.

With respect to people's satisfaction with local drinking water and air quality, see Robert E. Hurd, Apogee Market Strategies, "Consumer Attitude Survey on Water Quality Issues," 1993 (sponsored and published by the American Water Works Association Research Foundation, Denver, Colo.); the Wirthlin Report, "Research Supplement," August/September 1997, 1–2. A May 27, 1992, poll of 1,347 adults by CBS News found that 79 percent thought pollution was a "serious problem that's getting worse" in the country as a whole, but just 34 percent thought pollution was a serious problem in the area in which they lived. More generally, on the differences between people's perception of local versus national pollution conditions, see Everett Carll Ladd and Karlyn H. Bowman, *Attitudes Toward the Environment: Twenty-five Years After Earth Day* (Washington, D.C.: American Enterprise Institute for Public Policy Research, 1995), 47–48.

As regards people's different perceptions of crime at the local and national level, see Gallup Short Subjects, *Gallup Poll Monthly,* August 1996, 37; Dr. Garrett O'Keefe, principal investigator, *The Social Impact of the National Citizens' Crime Prevention Campaign,* Bureau of Justice Assistance Report NCJ 144533, U.S. Department of Justice, November 1993, 19, 23. Eighty-two percent of adults think crime in general is a "big problem in our society today," compared to just 17 percent who think crime is a big problem in their own community, I.C.R. Survey Research Group poll for the *Washington Post,* June–July 1996, released July 1996. Similarly, 81 percent of adults think teenage violence is a "big problem" in "most of the country," compared to 33 percent who think teen violence is a big problem in their community. "Crimes Committed by Youth: There's a Big Problem— Though It's Not as Bad 'in My Community,'" *Public Perspective,* June/July 1997, 32.

3. On people's differing perceptions of the state of their own jobs and finances versus that of the economy, see Everett Carll Ladd, "Thinking About America," *Public Perspective,* July/August 1993, 20; Ladd, "Big Swings in the National Mood Are a Staple of Contemporary Politics," *Public Perspective,* January/ February 1992, 4; and the historical graph charting people's personal reported levels of satisfaction with their job, future, and standard of living from 1963 to 1997, "Large Majorities Say They're Satisfied: With Their Jobs, Living Standards, Etc., and Their Future Prospects," *Public Perspective,* October/November 1997, 4.

With respect to Americans' perception that religion is declining in the United States, see the 1994 Mellman-Lazarus poll results cited in David Whitman, "I'm OK, You're Not," *U.S. News & World Report,* December 16, 1996, 26; and Lydia Saad, "Americans' Religious Commitment Affirmed: But Most Still Believe Religion Losing Influence," *Gallup Poll Monthly,* January 1996, 21–23.

In 1997, even after violent crime had continued a five-year-long decline, 67 percent of Americans believed violent crime was still increasing (45 percent said it was "increasing a lot"), according to a May 1, 1997, Louis Harris and Associates poll of 1,034 adults. The Harris poll was released on May 19, 1997. Several polls in 1997 also showed continued ambivalence about the economy, despite seven years of economic growth. A March–April 1997 Louis Harris and Associates poll (posted on Public Opinion Online on May 6, 1997) indicated 57 percent of the 1,006 adults questioned nationwide said they did "not feel good" about the country's economy; 40 percent said they did "feel good" about it. On people's satisfactions with their jobs, see also the 1997 *Wall Street Journal*/NBC News poll results reported in Ellen Graham, "Work May Be a Rat Race, but It's Not a Daily Grind," *Wall Street Journal,* September 19, 1997 (American Opinion section).

4. See Tom Brokaw, "The Brokaw Proposal: Fixing the System from the Ground Up," *Harvard International Journal of Press/Politics,* vol. 3, no. 1, Winter 1998, 5. Brokaw observed, "We're at peace. Crime is down, and the economy is up. . . . Nonetheless, there is this nagging anxiety. . . . We know there's a crisis of confidence in the traditional institutions of governance."

Brokaw's article is a slightly edited version of a keynote address he delivered at the John F. Kennedy School of Government, Harvard University, on May 9, 1997.

5. In 1997, people's personal satisfaction with their lives edged up to its highest level in the past 30 years. Forty-seven percent of Americans were highly contented with their lives, the highest figure since Gallup first asked a "ladder question" in 1964 asking people to rate their lives. (The ladder question states: "Imagine a ladder with steps numbered from zero at the bottom to 10 at the top. Suppose the top of the ladder represents the best possible life for you, and the bottom, the worst possible life for you. On which step of the ladder do you feel you personally stand at the present time?" Those who rated their lives between steps 8 and 10 were deemed highly satisfied.) Pew Research Center for the People & the Press, "Top 10 Stories of the Year; 1997: High Personal Contentment, Low News Interest," News release, December 22, 1997, 1.

6. Humphrey Taylor, "The Harris 'Feel Good' Index," Harris poll no. 21, May 5, 1997, 1–2.

7. Ibid., 1.

8. Ibid., 2.

For other overviews of recent polls demonstrating the I'm OK–They're Not syndrome, see Whitman, "I'm OK, You're Not," 24–32; Pew Research Center for the People & the Press, "The Optimism Gap Grows," news release, January 17, 1997; Susan Page, "The Mood at Inauguration," *USA Today*, January 17–19, 1997; Chuck Raasch, "The State of America on Inaugural Day: People Are More Satisfied," Gannett News Service, January 20, 1997; Charles Madigan, "The Optimism Gap," *Chicago Tribune*, March 4, 1997; Ellen Graham and Cynthia Crossen, "God, Motherhood, and Apple Pie," *Wall Street Journal*, December 13, 1996 (American Opinion section); Jeffrey L. Seglin, "The Happiest Workers in the World," *Inc.*, May 21, 1996; Frank Newport and Lydia Saad, "The Economy and the Election," *Public Perspective*, April/May 1996, 1–4; and John B. Judis, "Poll Position," *New Republic* (TRB column), March 4, 1996, 4.

9. Frank I. Luntz, "The State of the American Dream: Preliminary Findings," October 21, 1994 (study conducted for the Hudson Institute), August 11, 1994, questionnaire results, questions 1 and 6; Frank I. Luntz and Ron Dermer, "A Farewell to the American Dream?" *Public Perspective*, September/October 1994, 13.

10. Cross-tabulations provided by Steve Wagner and Jeffrey A. Minors, Luntz Research Companies, Arlington, Va.

11. Ed Goeas, interview with author, September 1995.

12. Chester Finn, Jr., interview with author, March 1995.

13. Elam et al., "The 28th Annual Phi Delta Kappa/Gallup Poll," 41–60; Elam, *How America Views Its Schools*, 9–16. For just two recent accounts of parents failing to support inner-city school reform, see Stephen Braun, "Learning Reform the Hard Way," *Los Angeles Times*, December 8, 1997, and Associated Press, "Unruly School Forces Principal to Back Down: Mass Suspensions Boomerang," reprinted in *Chicago Tribune*, November 21, 1997. Parents also often say they want more discipline in the classroom and opportunities for schooling—but object when their own child is disciplined, or when school officials try to lengthen the school year. See Lisa Arthur, "Support Fading for Year-Round Schools," *Miami Herald*, September 30, 1995.

14. O'Keefe, *The Social Impact of the National Citizens' Crime Prevention Campaign,* 80.

15. Polls routinely document Americans' excessive optimism about their own retirement prospects and their gloomy prognosis for other people's retirement prospects. While 68 percent of workers are somewhat or very confident that they will have enough money to live comfortably in retirement, only 6 percent believe that Americans other than themselves are saving enough to retire comfortably. "Big Dreams, Small Savings, Little Planning," 1997 Retirement Confidence Survey, October 16, 1997, news release, Washington, D.C. See Employee Benefit Research Institute, "Survey on Retirement Confidence, Wave VII-1997," Washington, D.C., 1997 and EBRI's "1997 Retirement Confidence Survey (RCS), Summary of Findings"; Steve Farkas and Jean Johnson, "Miles to Go: A Status Report on Americans' Plans for Retirement," Public Agenda, New York, N.Y., 1997, 27; and Ellen Graham, "Dreams of Cushy Retirement Clash with Meager Savings," *Wall Street Journal,* December 12, 1997 (American Opinion section).

16. See the polling data cited on page 2 of Donald F. Kettl and John J. DiIulio, Jr., *Cutting Government Waste* (Washington, D.C.: Brookings Institution, 1995).

17. Transcript of remarks of Lamar Alexander to the Governor's Conference on Business/Education Partnerships, Harrisburg, Pa., June 14, 1991, 8.

18. Hillary Rodham Clinton, "There Is No Such Thing as 'Other People's Children,'" *Los Angeles Times,* March 14, 1995.

19. Finn, interview with author.

20. Amy J. L. Baker, *Parents as School Partners Project: Final Report* (New York: National Council of Jewish Women Center for the Child, 1996), 1.

21. Maryland State Department of Education, Division of Planning, Results, and Information Management, *Maryland School Performance Report, 1994: State and School Systems,* 4–7, 28, 50–51.

22. Author's interviews with Garth Bowling, principal of John Hanson Middle School, May 1995, and Karla Schlaefli, chair of John Hanson PTSA in the 1994–95 school year, April 1995.

23. Maryland State Department of Education, *Maryland School Performance Report, 1995: School System and Schools—Charles County,* 5–8, 46–47; Maryland State Department of Education, *Maryland School Performance Report, 1997: School Systems and Schools—Charles County,* 8–10, 50–51.

Parents' ignorance about how their children fare academically compared to other kids is widespread. A 1997 poll of 700 parents by Public Agenda found only 7 percent of them knew "a lot" about how well their children's academic achievement compared with that of students abroad, 15 percent knew a lot about where their children stood in comparison with other youngsters in the United States, and 23 percent could say how their children stacked up against other children in their own state. Fewer than half the parents knew how their children compared with other students in the same grade. "Public Agenda: Reality Check," *Education Week,* January 8, 1998, 72, 74–75.

24. Schlaefli, interview with author.

25. Cindy Petrecca, interview with author, April 1995.

26. Roughly 75 percent of public school students and their parents believe their schools provide a good to excellent education, according to a survey of 1,000 parents with children attending public school in the third through twelfth grades. Louis Harris and Associates, *The American Teacher 1994—Violence in America's Public Schools: The Family Perspective,* New York (conducted for Metropolitan Life Insurance Company), fieldwork, April 22–May 19, 1994, 4. While comparatively fewer Americans send their children to private schools than in the recent past, many parents, when pressed, think the private schools do a better job than public schools. See the survey results reported in Jean Johnson, *Assignment Incomplete: The Unfinished Business of Education Reform,* New York, Public Agenda and the Institute for Educational Leadership, October 1995, 11–15.

27. Elam et al., "The 28th Annual Phi Delta Kappa/Gallup Poll."

28. Alexander, transcript of remarks to the Governor's Conference on Business/Education Partnerships, 8.

29. Almost 75 percent of parents think the amount of support shown by parents for their child's school is excellent or good, and just 8 percent think the level of support is poor. Louis Harris and Associates, *The American Teacher 1994,* 87. Polls showing that parents think their own parenting skills and school involvement surpass those of their parents include Bruskin Goldring Research, "OmniTel Parenting Study," Edison, N.J., September 1994, tables 2, 7, and 12. In the Bruskin Goldring survey, just 9 percent of the 655 parents surveyed said their parenting skills were "not as good" as those of their own parents, 5 percent admitted their parenting skills in terms of school activities weren't as good as their parents', and 3 percent said their parenting skills were not as good as their parents' when it came to discussing school problems. A May 1995 *Newsweek* poll of 803 parents with children under the age of 17 found that "seven out of 10 American fathers spend more time with their children than their own fathers did; nearly half think they are doing a better job and only 3 percent think they're worse." Moreover, 61 percent of today's dads said they understood their children better than their fathers did, and 55 percent said being a parent was more important to them than it was to their own fathers. Jerry Adler, "Building a Better Dad," *Newsweek,* June 17, 1996, 60–61.

Finally, a 1997 Princeton Survey Research Associates poll of 506 parents ages 18 to 44, with children ages 3 and under, found that just 4 percent of parents with toddlers thought they were worse parents then their own parents; 21 percent said they were "much better," 27 percent said they were better, and 46 percent rated themselves the "same" as their parents. "What Matters Most: A *Newsweek* Poll," *Newsweek* special issue on kids, May 1997, 9.

30. Louis Harris and Associates, *The American Teacher 1994,* 67–68.

31. June Kronholz, "Trying to Turn Around Their Schools, Americans Focus on the Role of Parents," *Wall Street Journal,* March 14, 1997 (American Opinion section). Results from the same poll are also in Ellen Graham, "We're Tough on Public Schools, but We Blame Our Families for Many of the Problems," *Wall Street Journal,* March 14, 1997 (American Opinion section).

The public's perception of parental disengagement from the schools has a sturdy basis in reality, particularly once students graduate from elementary school.

In 1996, just 47 percent of middle schools in the country reported that more than half of the parents of their pupils attended parent-teacher conferences during the school year. National Education Goals Panel, *The National Education Goals Report: Building a Nation of Learners, 1997* (Washington, D.C.: U.S. Government Printing Office, 1997), 65.

A recent decade-long study of more than 20,000 students in the 9th to 12th grades by psychology professor Laurence Steinberg documented an even more widespread lack of parental involvement in schools. More than half of students said they could bring home grades of C or worse without upsetting their parents; a quarter testified they could bring home grades of D or worse and not upset their parents. Close to a third of the high school students said their parents had no idea how they were doing in school. Most striking, more than 40 percent of the parents never attended a school program. Laurence Steinberg, *Beyond the Classroom: Why School Reform Has Failed and What Parents Need to Do* (New York: Simon & Schuster, 1996), 19–20, 42, 118–21.

32. The federal government's huge 1992 Survey of Income and Program Participation asked some 85,000 individuals to rate both the quality of education in local schools and the safety of local schools on a scale of 1 to 10—with 1 being the worst and 10 being the best. The median ratings of school safety (7.7) and quality of education in local schools (7.8) were virtually identical for nonpoor families and poor ones, and for poor families on welfare and other families. Maya Federman and David Levine, "Living Conditions of American Families," Council of Economic Advisors, White House, Washington, D.C., July 18, 1995, 22, table 1C.

33. A survey based on more than 50,000 responses from parents in Houston found that 90 percent believed public school teachers expected students to work hard, 81 percent felt school classrooms were clean and well organized, 78 percent believed that the schools provided the necessary instructional resources, and 75 percent thought the schools were safe. Houston Independent School District, "Student/Parent/Community Surveys, 1993–94, Districtwide and Administrative Area Results," Department of Research and Evaluation, 42–44. A poll of New Yorkers found that 52 percent of residents with children in public schools thought the city schools were good to excellent, compared to just 24 percent of residents citywide who thought city schools were good to excellent. EDK Associates, "Education Reform in New York City," prepared for Bank Street College of Education, August 1993, 6–8.

34. Cited in Casey Banas and Devonda Byers, "Chicago's Schools Hit as Worst," *Chicago Tribune,* November 7, 1987.

35. Cited in Dan A. Lewis and Kathryn Nakagawa, *Race and Educational Reform in the American Metropolis: A Study of School Decentralization* (Albany, N.Y.: State University of New York Press, 1995), 102.

36. Ibid., 132.

37. Dan Lewis, interview with author, April 1995.

38. Lewis and Nakagawa, *Race and Educational Reform,* 103–7.

39. Ibid., 109–22. The record of urban school parents may be even worse than that of parents elsewhere. In a 1988 report on urban schooling, the Carnegie

Foundation found that in a New Orleans high school that required parents to pick up report cards, 70 percent of the report cards remained unclaimed two months after the marking period. Cited in Leon Botstein, *Jefferson's Children* (New York: Doubleday, 1997).

In 1995, the Illinois General Assembly enacted another round of school reform that shifted control away from parents and turned the schools over to Chicago mayor Richard M. Daley and his handpicked school board superintendent Paul Vallas. Vallas soon placed 109 public schools on academic probation for their poor performance. Edward Walsh, "Chicago Puts 109 Schools on Probation; Principals May Face Dismissal," *Washington Post,* October 2, 1996. By 1997, graduation and attendance rates in Chicago's school had risen to their highest levels in a decade, and there were some preliminary signs that test scores were rising. President Clinton hailed this most recent round of school reform by saying, "I want what is happening in Chicago to happen all over America." Stephen Braun, "Learning Reform the Hard Way," *Los Angeles Times,* December 8, 1997.

40. Mark J. Penn, interview with author, November 1996.

41. "On Target," *Newsweek,* November 18, 1996, 48.

42. Todd S. Purdum, "Clinton Plans to Lift Public out of 'Funk,'" *New York Times,* September 24, 1995.

43. Mark J. Penn, "The Mandate for the Middle," Penn & Schoen Associates, undated, 13; James Bennet, "The Exit Polls: Voter Interviews Suggest Clinton Was Persuasive on Path of U.S.," *New York Times,* November 6, 1996; Ronald G. Shafer, "Washington Wire," *Wall Street Journal,* October 25, 1996.

44. Ibid.

45. Purdum, "Clinton Plans to Lift Public Out of 'Funk.'"

46. "Survey of Americans and Economists on the Economy," sponsored by the *Washington Post*/Kaiser Family Foundation/Harvard University Survey Project, Henry J. Kaiser Family Foundation, Menlo Park, Calif., October 1996, 14; Pew Research Center for the People & the Press, "What Budget Agreement? Americans Only a Little Better Off, but Much Less Anxious," news release, May 23, 1997, Washington, D.C., 1, 15–19.

47. October 17–20, 1996, poll of 1,479 adults for *CBS News/New York Times,* retrieved from Public Opinion Online, Roper Center for Public Opinion Research, University of Connecticut at Storrs, load date June 13, 1997.

48. Karlyn H. Bowman, *The 1993–94 Debate on Health Care Reform* (Washington, D.C.: AEI Press, 1994), 6–7. Jacobs and Shapiro, "The Conventional Wisdom," report even slightly higher numbers over a 10-year period, with 84 to 88 percent of people expressing satisfaction with the quality of care they get from doctors, 23.

49. Daniel Yankelovich, "The Debate That Wasn't: The Public and the Clinton Plan," *Health Affairs,* spring 1995, 13–14, 16.

50. John Immerwahr, interview with author, May 1995.

51. David W. Moore, "Polling on Health Care and Medicare: Continuity in Public Opinion," *Public Perspective,* October/November 1995, 13–15.

52. Ibid.

53. Yankelovich, "The Debate That Wasn't," 11.

54. Columbia Institute, "What Shapes Lawmakers' Views: A Survey of Members of Congress and Key Staff on Health Care Reform" (study conducted for the Henry J. Kaiser Family Foundation and the Harvard School of Public Health), Washington, D.C., released May 15, 1995, fieldwork, December 1994–February 1995, 9, 16–17. Dr. Orval Hansen of the Columbia Institute interviewed 38 members of the U.S. House of Representatives and Senate, and 18 legislative staff members.

55. James Fallows, *Breaking the News* (New York: Pantheon Books, 1996), 219.

56. Kathleen Hall Jamieson, "When Harry Met Louise," *Washington Post*, August 15, 1994.

57. Robert J. Blendon, interview with author, April 1995.

58. Advance copy of Robert J. Blendon, Mollyann Brodie, and John M. Benson, "Whatever Happened to Americans' Support for the Clinton Health Plan?" Harvard School of Public Health (published in summer 1995 issue of *Health Affairs*), table 2. Blendon et al. provide a breakdown of polling data from a Gallup poll conducted for CNN/*USA Today*, dated April 16, 1994. Bowman, *The 1993–94 Debate on Health Care Reform*, 28–30.

59. Yankelovich, "The Debate That Wasn't," 14–15.

60. Ibid.

61. February 1994 Princeton Survey Research Associates poll for the Harvard Program, cited in Bowman, *The 1993–94 Debate on Health Care Reform*, 37.

62. Richard Morin and Dan Balz, "Americans Losing Trust in Each Other and Institutions," *Washington Post*, January 28, 1996.

63. Kathleen Hall Jamieson and Joseph N. Cappella, "Do Health Reform Polls Clarify or Confuse the Public?" *Journal of American Health Policy*, May/June 1994, 39; Fallows, *Breaking the News*, 226. See also Joseph N. Cappella and Kathleen Hall Jamieson, *Spiral of Cynicism: The Press and the Public Good* (New York and Oxford, England: Oxford University Press, 1997).

64. Blendon et al., "Whatever Happened to Americans' Support?" 7.

65. Robert J. Blendon and John M. Benson, "Making Major Changes in the Health Care System: Public Opinion Parallels Between Two Recent Debates," Harvard School of Public Health, undated; David W. Moore, "Public Opposes Republican Plan to Change Medicare," *Gallup Poll Monthly*, September 1995, 14–16; Robert J. Blendon et al., "The Public's View of the Future of Medicare," *JAMA*, vol. 274, no. 20 (November 22–29, 1995), 1645–1648.

66. Blendon and Benson, "Making Major Changes in the Health Care System," 2–4; Moore, "Public Opposes Republican Plan," 14.

67. Pew Research Center for the People & the Press, "What Budget Agreement?" 3.

68. Robert J. Blendon, interview with author, January 1996.

CHAPTER TWO: The Roots of the Optimism Gap

1. Tom Wolfe, "Aspirations of an American Century," *Advertising Age*, June 12, 1989, 14.

2. "Over the 1970s, Assessments Worsened Markedly," *Public Perspective,*

October/November 1995, 30. By 1994, almost every demographic group believed the nation's schools were in decline. Mellman-Lazarus-Lake, "AASA Nationwide Survey: Analysis of Findings" (executive summary), Washington, D.C., January 1994, 15.

3. Daniel Yankelovich, "How Changes in the Economy Are Reshaping American Values," in Henry J. Aaron, "Thomas E. Mann, and Timothy Taylor, eds., *Values and Public Policy* (Washington, D.C.: Brookings Institution, 1994), 25.

4. "Opinion Pulse: Television's Credibility . . . ," *American Enterprise,* September/October 1997, 92.

5. Craig Calhoun, "Indirect Relationships and Imagined Communities: Large-Scale Social Integration and the Transformation of Everyday Life," in Pierre Bourdieu and James S. Coleman, eds., *Social Theory for a Changing Society* (Boulder, Colo.: Westview Press, 1991), 112.

The neoconservative Irving Kristol offers another explanation for Americans' pessimism about the future, especially their pessimism about the prospects for the next generation. He believes that the United States is no longer a nation of immigrants that nurtures inevitable hopes of upward mobility. Kristol acknowledges that people's "confidence has eroded, but that is a perfectly natural phenomenon, not any kind of crisis. The reason it is perfectly natural is that it is a matter of arithmetic, and the laws of arithmetic bow before no dream. What we call the American Dream are the expectations evoked in the hearts and minds of a nation of immigrants. . . . But the United States is no longer a nation of immigrants—a fact obscured by the current controversy over the rate of immigration today. We are merely a nation descended from former immigrants. We are no longer a 'new' nation but a mature one, populated by the second, third, fourth and fifth generations of Americans. And in such mature nations, upward social and economic mobility is not a generational phenomenon but a rather haphazard individual one." Irving Kristol, "America Dreaming," column distributed by the American Enterprise Institute, Washington, D.C., September 1995.

6. John W. Wright, ed., *The Universal Almanac, 1997* (Kansas City: Andrews and McMeel, 1996), 235. By comparison, in 1971 the average household with a television had one television on six hours a day, two hours less than in 1995.

7. U.S. Bureau of the Census, *Statistical Abstract of the United States, 1997* (Washington, D.C., National Technical Information Service, 1997), 566.

8. Ibid.

9. George Gerbner, "Marketing Global Mayhem," *The Public,* vol. 2 (1995), 2, 73.

10. George Gerbner, "Television's Influence on Values and Behavior," *Weekly Psychiatry Update Series,* lesson 24, vol. 2 (Princeton, N.J. and New York, N.Y.: Biomedia, undated), 6.

11. S. Robert Lichter, Linda S. Lichter, and Stanley Rothman, *Prime Time: How TV Portrays American Culture* (Washington, D.C.: Regnery, 1994), 299.

12. S. Robert Lichter, interview with author, February 1996.

13. Stephen Seplow and Jonathan Storm, "TV and Kids: A Brighter Picture," *Philadelphia Inquirer,* December 3, 1997.

14. Aletha C. Huston et al., *Big World, Small Screen: The Role of Television in American Society* (Lincoln, Nebr.: University of Nebraska Press, 1992), 70.

15. Joseph Turow, *Breaking Up America* (Chicago: University of Chicago Press, 1997), 4.

16. Ibid., 7.

17. Robert J. Samuelson, *The Good Life and Its Discontents: The American Dream in the Age of Entitlement, 1945–1995* (New York: Times Books, 1995), 210–11.

18. Ibid., 72. When Johnson launched the War on Poverty, he pledged: "This administration today, here and now, declares unconditional war on poverty in America . . . It will not be a short or easy struggle, but we shall not rest until that war is won. . . . Our aim is not only to relieve the symptom of poverty, but to cure it and, above all, to prevent it." See Johnson's 1964 State of the Union. "Annual Message to the Congress on the State of the Union, January 8, 1964," *Public Papers of the Presidents* (Washington, D.C.: U.S. Government Printing Office, 1965), 91. At a 1966 hearing, Sargent Shriver, the head of LBJ's antipoverty program, estimated that it would take "about 10 years" to win the War on Poverty. Malcolm Gladwell, "The Failure of Our Best Intentions," *Washington Post,* December 3, 1995.

19. *Economic Report of the President and the Annual Report of the Council of Economic Advisers* (Washington, D.C.: U.S. Government Printing Office, 1997), table B-29, 333.

20. Quoted in Stanley Lebergott, *Pursuing Happiness: American Consumers in the Twentieth Century* (Princeton, N.J.: Princeton University Press, 1993), 69.

21. Yankelovich, "How Changes in the Economy Are Reshaping American Values," 38–39.

22. Roper Starch Worldwide, "The Boomer Balancing Act: Baby Boomers Talk About Life and the American Dream" (sponsored by FirstWave), August 1996, 6, 38–41. Roper Starch Worldwide surveyed 1,001 adults, ages 32 to 50, during June 1996.

23. "The Possessions Paradox," *Public Pulse,* vol. 10, no. 7 (July 1995), Roper Starch Worldwide, 2–3.

24. Everett Carll Ladd and George Pettinico, "Personal Financial Achievements and Status: A *Reader's Digest* National Survey, July 18–30, 1996, Survey Results," Roper Center for Public Opinion Research, University of Connecticut at Storrs, 1996, 2.

25. Ibid., 19, 22.

26. Ibid., 22.

27. Ibid.

28. "The National Prospect: A Symposium," *Commentary,* November 1995. James Q. Wilson's contribution is on pages 112–13.

The neoconservative Midge Decter takes a similar tone when she observes: "Children have seldom in history been so much attended to and so kindly treated as ours. . . . the lives we lead are in respect of ease and comfort and confidence and good health simply unprecedented. Never have so many, even the poor among us, had so much. We are disoriented. We do not know whether to laugh or to cry; we do not know whom or what to thank; and we cannot think of what there might be to want next. And so we giggle and preen and complain and forget our debts and keep on seeking for things (and sometimes finding them)." Midge Decter, "Affluence and Divorce," *Public Interest,* spring 1997, 119.

29. Adam Smith, *The Wealth of Nations,* originally published in 1776 (New York: Knopf, Everyman's Library, 1991 ed.), 96.

30. Robert H. Frank and Phillip J. Cook, *The Winner-Take-All Society* (New York: Free Press, Martin Kessler Books, 1995), 103–5.

31. Survey results from Northeastern University's Center for the Study of Sport in Society, cited in John Simons, "Improbable Dreams," *U.S. News & World Report,* March 24, 1997, 46. See also the results of the 1997 poll sponsored by *Sports Illustrated,* reported in "Too Single-minded?" *Sports Illustrated,* December 8, 1997, 42, 51.

32. Simons, "Improbable Dreams," 46–51.

33. See the studies cited in David G. Myers, *Social Psychology,* 2nd ed. (New York: McGraw-Hill, 1987), 96.

34. Carolyn Kay Brancato, "New Corporate Performance Measures," The Conference Board, New York, Report Number 1118-95-RR, 1995, executive summary, 9; Laurie Larwood and William Whittaker, "Managerial Myopia: Self-Serving Biases in Organizational Planning," *Journal of Applied Psychology,* vol. 62, no. 2 (1977), 194–98.

35. Hillary Rodham Clinton, *It Takes a Village* (New York: Simon & Schuster, 1996), 227.

36. Cost, Quality, and Child Outcomes Study Team, *Cost, Quality, and Child Outcomes in Child Care Centers. Public Report,* Economics Department, University of Colorado at Denver, 1995, 69.

Americans have long been satisfied with their child care arrangements. The 1975 National Child Care Consumer Study found that 94 percent of all parents were "very satisfied" or "satisfied" with their current child care arrangements. The 1990 National Child Care Survey, which conducted almost 4,400 interviews with parents whose children were age 12 or under, found 96 percent were "very satisfied" or "satisfied," too. Sandra L. Hofferth et al., *National Child Care Survey, 1990* (Washington, D.C.: Urban Institute Press, 1991), Urban Institute Report 91–5, 14, 17, 232. A companion survey of 973 low-income families found 95 percent of those who used some form of supplemental care for children under the age of 5 were satisfied or highly satisfied. April A. Brayfield et al., *Caring for Children in Low-Income Families: A Substudy of the National Child Care Survey, 1990* (Washington, D.C.: Urban Institute Press, 1993), Urban Institute Report 93-2, 8, 80.

37. Cost, Quality, and Child Outcomes Study Team, *Cost, Quality, and Child Outcomes in Child Care Centers,* 70.

38. Clinton, *It Takes a Village,* 231–32.

39. Earvin "Magic" Johnson with William Novak, *My Life* (New York: Ballantine Books, 1992), 318.

40. Earvin "Magic" Johnson, "HIV Has Forced Me to Retire, but I'll Still Enjoy Life as I Speak Out About Safe Sex," *Sports Illustrated,* November 19, 1991, 19.

Several psychologists and psychiatrists have studied the impact of Magic Johnson's announcement that he had the HIV virus on public attitudes and preventive behavior. The announcement spurred an initial rash of calls to AIDS hotlines but seems to have had little long-term impact, even among youth who idolized the Lakers superstar. See Seth Kalichman and Tricia L. Hunter, "The Disclosure of Celebrity HIV Infection: Its Effects on Public Attitudes," *American Journal of Public Health,* vol. 82, no. 10 (October 1992), 1,374–1,376; Carol K. Sigelman et al., "Do You Believe in Magic? The Impact of 'Magic' Johnson on Adolescents' AIDS Knowledge and Attitudes," *AIDS Education and Prevention,* vol. 5, no. 2 (1993), 153–61; Seth C. Kalichman et al., "Earvin 'Magic' Johnson's HIV Serostatus Disclosure: Effects on Men's Perceptions of AIDS," *Journal of Consulting and Clinical Psychology,* vol. 61, no. 5 (1993), 887–91; and Seth. C. Kalichman, "Magic Johnson and Public Attitudes Toward AIDS: A Review of Empirical Findings," *AIDS Education and Prevention* vol. 6, no. 6 (1994), 542–57.

41. Kelly Kurt (Associated Press), "Morrison: 'I Thought I Was Bulletproof . . . ,'" *Washington Times,* February 16, 1996.

42. See, generally, Neil D. Weinstein and William M. Klein, "Resistance of Personal Risk Perceptions to Debiasing Interventions," *Health Psychology,* vol. 14, no. 2 (1995), 132–40; Neil D. Weinstein, "Unrealistic Optimism About Susceptibility to Health Problems: Conclusions from a Community-Wide Sample," *Journal of Behavioral Medicine,* vol. 10, no. 5, (1987), 481–500; and Susan Moses, "The Role of Mass Media in Deterring Tobacco and Alcohol Use Among Children and Adolescents," Center for Health Communication, Harvard School of Public Health, submitted to the Robert Wood Johnson Foundation, December 1991.

With respect to women's self-perceived immunity to pregnancy, see Meg Gerrard and C. A. Elizabeth Lucus, "Judgements of Vulnerability to Pregnancy: The Role of Risk Factors and Individual Differences," *Personality and Social Psychology Bulletin,* vol. 21, no. 2 (February 1995), 160; Jerry Burger and Linda Burns, "The Illusion of Unique Invulnerability and the Use of Effective Contraception," *Personality and Social Psychology Bulletin,* vol. 14, no. 2 (June 1988), 264–270; and Bernard E. Whitley, Jr., and Andrea L. Hern, "Perception of Vulnerability to Pregnancy and the Use of Effective Contraception," *Personality and Social Psychology Bulletin,* vol. 17, no. 1 (February 1991), 104–10.

On self-perception of smoking risks, see S. C. Segerstrom et al., "Optimistic Bias Among Cigarette Smokers," *Journal of Applied Social Psychology,* vol. 23, (1993), 1,606; Simon Chapman et al., "Self-Exempting Beliefs About Smoking and Health: Differences Between Smokers and Ex-smokers," *American Journal of Public Health,* vol. 83 (February 1993), 215–19; William B. Hansen and C. K. Malotte, "Perceived Personal Immunity: The Development of Beliefs About Susceptibility to the Consequences of Smoking," *Preventive Medicine,* vol. 15 (1986), 363–72; and Alfred McAlister et al., "Antismoking Campaigns: Progress in the Application of Social Learning Theory," in Ronald E. Rice and Charles K. Atkin, eds., *Public Communication Campaigns,* 2nd ed. (Newbury Park, Calif.: Sage Publication, 1989), 293–307.

With regard to Americans' perception of drinking risks, see William B. Hansen et al., "Perceived Personal Immunity to the Consequences of Drinking Alcohol: The Relationship Between Behavior and Perception," *Journal of Behavioral Medicine,* vol. 14, no. 3 (1991), 1991, 205–23.

College students vastly overestimate how much other students drink, and their misperceptions seem to create a self-fulfilling prophecy, i.e., their understanding that most fellow students regularly binge drink appears to lead them to binge drink themselves. See H. Wesley Perkins, "College Student Misperceptions of Alcohol and Other Drug Norms among Peers" in U.S. Department of Education, *Designing Alcohol and Other Drug Prevention Programs in Higher Education* (Newton, Mass.: The Higher Education Center for Alcohol and other Drug Prevention, 1997), 177–206.

Finally, there is a large literature about people's unrealistic optimism about AIDS. See J. B. Pryor and G. Reeder, eds., *The Social Psychology of AIDS Infection* (Hillsdale, N.J.: Lawrence Erlbaum, 1993), chaps. 1–3. Other studies include Frank W. van der Velde et al., "Perceiving AIDS-Related Risk: Accuracy as a Function of Differences in Actual Risk," *Health Psychology,* vol. 13, no. 1 (1994), 25–33; Seth C. Kalichman et al., "Perceptions of AIDS Susceptibility Among Minority and Nonminority Women at Risk for HIV Infection," *Journal of Consulting and Clinical Psychology,* vol. 60, no. 5 (1991), 725–32; and Shelley E. Taylor et al., "Optimism, Coping, Psychological Distress, and High-Risk Sexual Behavior Among Men at Risk for Acquired Immunodeficiency Syndrome (AIDS)," *Journal of Personality and Social Psychology,* vol. 63, no. 3 (1992), 460–73.

43. David McKirnan, interview with author, April 1995.

44. The 1990–91 survey sampled just over 8,000 people in "high-risk" cities. Daniel C. Berrios et al., "HIV Antibody Testing Among Those at Risk for Infection: The National AIDS Behavioral Surveys," *JAMA,* vol. 270, no. 13 (October 6, 1993), 1,576. Even in more recent years, a shockingly large number of HIV-positive men and women have not been disclosing their HIV status to their lovers, or regularly using condoms. A study done from 1994 to 1996 at Boston City Hospital and Rhode Island Hospital's HIV clinic in Providence found that 40 percent of sexually active HIV-positive patients new to medical care had not disclosed they had the AIDS virus to all their sexual partners in the prior six months; among those who did disclose they were HIV infected, only 42 percent used condoms all the time. Michael D. Stein et al., "Disclosure of HIV-Positive Status to Partners," *Archives of Internal Medicine,* vol. 158, February 9, 1998, 253–257.

45. Mac W. Otten, Jr., et al., "High Rate of HIV Seroconversion Among Patients Attending Urban Sexually Transmitted Disease Clinics," *AIDS,* vol. 8, no. 4 (1994), 549–53.

46. Mac W. Otten, Jr., et al., "Changes in Sexually Transmitted Disease Rates After HIV Testing and Posttest Counseling, Miami, 1988 to 1989," *American Journal of Public Health,* vol. 83, no. 4 (April 1993), 529–32.

47. Terry Tucker, interview with author, April 1995.

48. Bruce Heath, interview with author, April 1995.

49. Kirk Arthur, interview with author, April 1995.

CHAPTER THREE: The Self-Admiring American

1. Adam Smith, *The Wealth of Nations,* originally published in 1776 (New York: Knopf, Everyman's Library, 1991 ed.), 95–96.

2. The findings of the *U.S. News & World Report* poll of 1,000 adults are

briefly discussed in Douglas Stanglin, "Oprah: A Heavenly Body," Washington Whispers, *U.S. News & World Report,* March 31, 1997, 18. A fuller recounting of the results is in Market Facts, Telenation poll tabulations, data collected March 10–12, 1997; and unpublished memoranda on the "Heaven Poll" to *U.S. News & World Report* from Lori Gudermuth of the Tarrance Group (March 16, 1997), and from Celinda Lake and Dana Stanley of Lake Sosin Snell & Associates (March 17, 1997).

3. Leslie McAneny, "A Fourth of All Americans 'Most Admire' Mother Teresa," *Gallup Poll Monthly,* December 1996, 10.

4. Cynthia Crossen, "Rate Your Own Morals and Values on a Scale from One to 100 (100 Being Perfect)," *Wall Street Journal,* December 13, 1996 (American Opinion section).

An October 1995 survey by GOP pollster Frank Luntz asked 1,581 adults, "Are you a better person morally than most of the people around you?" Fifty-eight percent responded yes, they were superior, and another 14 percent said they were the moral equals of most people around them. Just 24 percent said they did not think they were morally superior to most others. Data supplied by Luntz Research and Strategic Services, Arlington, Va.

5. Cited in Thomas Gilovich, *How We Know What Isn't So* (New York: Free Press, 1991), 75. Julius Caesar had much the same thought when he said, "Men are nearly always willing to believe what they wish." *De Bello Gallico,* bk. 3, sec. 18.

6. R. S. Uhrbock, "Personal Estimates of Character Traits," *Pedagogical Seminary,* vol. 33 (1926), 491–96. Uhrbock's research is summarized in Ruth C. Wylie, *The Self-Concept,* revised ed., vol. 2 (Lincoln, Nebr.: University of Nebraska Press, 1979 ed.), 676.

7. Paul Torrance, "Rationalizations About Test Performance as a Function of Self-Concepts," *Journal of Social Psychology,* vol. 39 (May 1954), 211–17.

8. Orville G. Brim, Jr., John Neuligner, and David C. Glass, "Experiences and Attitudes of American Adults Concerning Standardized Intelligence Tests," Technical Report No. 1 on the Social Consequences of Testing, Russell Sage Foundation, New York, 1965, iii, 3, 21–22, 32–34, 42, 119–20.

9. K. Patricia Cross, "Not *Can,* but *Will* College Teaching Be Improved?" in John A. Centra, ed., *Renewing and Evaluating Teaching: New Directions for Higher Education* (San Francisco: Jossey-Bass, 1977), 10. Cross's analysis was based on the responses of almost 600 faculty members.

10. Robert T. Blackburn et al., "Are Instructional Improvement Programs Off-Target?" *Current Issues in Higher Education* vol. 1 (1980), 32–48.

11. Ibid., 47.

12. Arthur Levine, *When Dreams and Heroes Died* (San Francisco: Jossey-Bass, 1980), 103–5.

13. William James, *The Varieties of Religious Experience,* quoted in Lionel Tiger, *Optimism: The Biology of Hope* (New York: Simon & Schuster, 1979), 26.

14. Ed Marciniak, *Reclaiming the Inner City* (Washington, D.C.: National Center for Urban Ethnic Affairs, 1986), 63, 69.

15. Edward Walsh, "Chicago Tries to Replace 'Castle' with Community," *Washington Post,* October 28, 1995.

16. Elizabeth Gleick, "Belated Outrage for Girl X," *Time,* February 24, 1997, 31; Eric Ferkenhoff and Dahleen Glanton, "Suspect Arrested in Girl X Assault," *Chicago Tribune,* April 4, 1997.

17. Vincent Lane, interview with author, April 1995.

18. The high-rise graveyard analogy comes from Stephen Braun, "New Life for Notorious High-Rises?" *Los Angeles Times,* June 2, 1994; the "hell on earth" moniker is cited in Marciniak, *Reclaiming the Inner City,* 63.

19. Metropolitan Planning Council, "Untapped Potentials: The Capacities, Needs, and Views of Chicago's Highrise Public Housing Residents," Task Force on CHA Rehabilitation and Reinvestment (project director, Gwendolyn Clemons), September 1986, 1, 7, 15, 46.

20. Joyce Flake, interview with author, April 1995.

21. Willie Bell Harris, interview with author, April 1995.

22. Joyce Flake, interview with author, December 1996.

23. Several outside observers who have spent time in Chicago's high-rise projects have reported that a substantial number of residents share a sense of community and are not eager to move. See Sudhir Alladi Venkatesh, "An Invisible Community: Inside Chicago's Public Housing," *American Prospect,* no. 34 (September/October 1997), 35–40; Jonathan Eig, "House Hunting," *New Republic,* December 1, 1997, 17–18; Documentary filmmaker Frederick Wiseman's comments about his PBS film *Public Housing* on the Ida B. Wells Homes in Chicago, in "Searching for Hope in 'Public Housing,' " *Washington Post,* November 28, 1997; Cory Oldweiler, "Cabrini Changes Come All Too Slowly," *The Chicago Reporter,* March 1998; and Marciniak, *Reclaiming the Inner City,* 64–65, 91–94.

In 1993–94, the Center for Urban Affairs and Policy Research at Northwestern University surveyed more than 400 residents of the Dearborn Homes, a series of mid-rise family housing projects on Chicago's South Side. Two in three residents said they were satisfied with their community in general, and 71 percent felt that their neighbors were friendly people. Almost half of the tenants said they talked with one of their neighbors on a daily basis, and about 70 percent did so at least once a week. Three in four residents said that they liked their apartment. A quarter of the residents said they wanted to remain permanently at Dearborn, while another 43 percent said they weren't sure whether they would stay permanently at the housing complex. Deborah Puntenney, "Developing Internal Markets: The Results of a Survey of Dearborn Homes Residents on Community Economic Development Issues," final report, Center for Urban Affairs and Policy Research, Northwestern University, Evanston, Ill., 1994, 67–70. A 1994 survey of 517 residents of the ABLA, Henry Horner, and Rockwell Gardens public housing developments in Chicago also found substantial residential stability: One in three tenants had lived in CHA housing for 16 years or more. Toni Henle, "Work, Education, and Training: Experiences and Preferences of Public Housing Residents at ABLA, Horner, and Rockwell Housing Developments," Center for Urban Economic Development, University of Illinois at Chicago, Project 395, January 1995, 10.

The biannual American Housing Survey, run by the Census Bureau, asks some 150,000 household heads both to rate the quality of their neighborhoods on a scale of 1 to 10 and to identify neighborhood problems. Inner-city households are more likely to identify neighborhood problems and less likely to give high ratings than households in other areas, yet most inner-city residents seem relatively satisfied. In 1993, just over half of the nation's central-city residents failed to cite any problems with neighborhood conditions. On a scale of 1 to 10, with 10 being the best, 24 percent of central-city residents gave their neighborhood an overall ranking of 10, and another 48 percent gave it a ranking of 7 to 9. U.S. Department of Commerce, Bureau of the Census, *American Housing Survey for the United States in 1993: 20th Anniversary Edition of the AHS,* Current Housing Reports, H150/93, February 1995, table 8-8, 383.

News accounts relentlessly portray public housing high-rises as a kind of killing fields, but the evidence that high-rises have exceedingly high rates of violent crime is more mixed than the coverage might suggest. The 1995 National Crime Victimization Survey shows that black urban residents of public housing were only slightly more likely to have been the victims of a violent crime that year than urban whites who did not live in public housing (10 percent compared to 7.2 percent), and were actually slightly less likely to have suffered from property crime (22.3 percent compared to 23.9 percent). Asked specifically in the 1995 American Housing Survey, "Does the neighborhood have neighborhood crime?," 49 percent of blacks who lived in public housing said the neighborhood did not have crime. An additional 15 percent said that while local crime existed, they were not bothered by it. See Carol J. DeFrances and Steven K. Smith, "Perceptions of Neighborhood Crime, 1995," Bureau of Justice Statistics Special Report, U.S. Department of Justice, NCJ-165811, April 1998, 7, 9. New York City's public housing, which has a reputation for being well run, has lower reported rates of crime than other parts of the city. John DeSantis, "On the Beat in the Projects: N.Y. Housing Police Raise Quality of Life," *Washington Times,* April 8, 1994; see also Terence Dunworth and Aaron Saiger, "Drugs and Crime in Public Housing: A Three-City Analysis," a final summary report presented to the National Institute of Justice, U.S. Department of Justice, March 1994, Report NCJ 145329.

Just like some of the tenants at Cabrini-Green, residents of other high-rise projects sometimes report feeling safer than residents of surrounding areas. For surveys of public housing residents' beliefs about local crime, see Harold R. Holzman et al., "Revisiting the Relationship Between Crime and Architectural Design: An Analysis of Data from HUD's 1994 Survey of Public Housing Residents," *Cityscape: A Journal of Policy Development and Research,* vol. 2, no. 1 (February 1996), 107–26; Harvey Zelon et al., "Survey of Public Housing Residents: Crime and Crime Prevention in Public Housing," Research Triangle Institute, Research Triangle Park, North Carolina, prepared for U.S. Department of Housing and Urban Development, July 15, 1994; and William M. Rohe and Raymond J. Burby, "Fear of Crime in Public Housing," *Environment and Behavior,* vol. 20, no. 6 (November 1998), 700–720.

24. Lane, interview with author.

25. Shelley E. Taylor, *Positive Illusions* (New York: Basic Books, 1989), 33.

26. Tiger, *Optimism,* 35.

27. Quoted in Gilovich, *How We Know What Isn't So,* 84.

28. David G. Myers, *Social Psychology,* 2nd ed. (New York: McGraw-Hill, 1987), 99.

29. Professor Neil Weinstein of the Department of Human Ecology, Rutgers University, New Brunswick, N.J., maintains a bibliography of studies on perceptions of invulnerability and optimistic biases called "Optimistic Biases About Risk and Future Life Events." As of April 1994, the bibliography listed more than 200 papers and studies.

30. Gilovich, *How We Know What Isn't So,* 77.

31. Taylor, *Positive Illusions,* 33.

32. Neil D. Weinstein, "Unrealistic Optimism About Susceptibility to Health Problems: Conclusions from a Community-Wide Sample," *Journal of Behavioral Medicine,* vol. 10, no. 5 (1987), 481–500. Weinstein surveyed 296 adults in New Brunswick, N.J.

33. Paul Sparks and Richard Sheperd, "Public Perceptions of the Potential Hazards Associated with Food Production and Food Consumption: An Empirical Study," *Risk Analysis,* vol. 15, no. 5 (1994), 802.

34. Taylor, *Positive Illusions,* 36; Weinstein, "Unrealistic Optimism," 496.

35. Gilovich, *How We Know What Isn't So,* 84; Wylie, *The Self-Concept,* 679; "Today's Student Rates Him/Herself Pretty Highly," *Public Perspective,* October/November 1995, 38.

36. Unpublished memorandum on the "Heaven Poll" to *U.S. News & World Report* from Lake and Stanley, 2.

37. J. B. Pryor and G. Reeder, ed., *The Social Psychology of AIDS Infection* (Hillsdale, N.J.: Lawrence Erlbaum, 1993), 24.

38. Meg Gerrard and Teddy D. Warner, "Comparison of Marine and College Women's HIV/AIDS-Relevant Sexual Behaviors," Department of Psychology, Iowa State University, undated paper, table 2, 31. The authors surveyed 432 sexually experienced female marines.

39. Cited in *Dictionary of Quotations,* collected and arranged by Bergen Evans (New York: Delacorte Press, 1968).

40. Daniel Katz et al., *Bureaucratic Encounters* (Ann Arbor, Mich.: Survey Research Center, Institute for Social Research, University of Michigan, 1975), 4, 120.

41. Ibid., 128–29.

42. Kay Lehman Schlozman and Sidney Verba, *Injury to Insult: Unemployment, Class, and Political Response* (Cambridge, Mass.: Harvard University Press, 1979), 153.

43. Michael S. Lewis-Beck, *Economics and Elections* (Ann Arbor, Mich.: University of Michigan Press, 1988), 133–35. On the paradox of Reagan's popularity in 1984—despite the effects of the withering 1981–82 recession—see also D. Roderick Kiewiet and Douglas Rivers, "The Economic Basis of Reagan's Appeal," in John E. Chubb and Paul E. Peterson, eds., *The New Direction in American Politics* (Washington, D.C.: Brookings Institution, 1985), 69–90. Political scientist Diana Mutz has shown that while "losing a job has an inescapable impact on an individual's everyday life . . . reading about unemployment in a newspaper may have greater consequences for U.S. political life." Diana C. Mutz, "Mass Media

and the Depoliticization of Personal Experience," *American Journal of Political Science,* vol. 36, no. 2, May 1992, 502–503.

44. See, generally, the references for notes 2 and 3, chap. 1.

On the subject of race, one in three Americans think the problem of racial discrimination against blacks is "somewhat serious" (23 percent) or "very serious" (10 percent) in the area where they live. But nearly three in four think racial discrimination against blacks is somewhat serious (47 percent) or very serious (25 percent) in the United States as a whole. "Gallup Short Subjects," *Gallup Poll Monthly,* July 1996, 42.

In 1985, the *Los Angeles Times* asked 2,600 adults, "Just your best guess, what is the percentage of people in this country who have been a victim of child sexual abuse at some time in their lives?" Three in five respondents guessed that between 21 and 80 percent of Americans had been sexually abused as kids. When asked what percentage of children in the local community had been sexually abused, the numbers plummeted. Two in three people thought that less than 20 percent of local kids had been abused. Unpublished poll tabulations for July 1985 poll, tables 11 and 12. In Washington State, residents believe that child abuse and neglect are widespread and the rate is increasing statewide, but they think the child abuse and neglect rate is lower in their communities and is not rising. Richard Brandon and Andrew Gordon, "Public Opinion About Child Protection Issues in Washington State: Executive Summary of Public Opinion Research" (polling of 1,300 individuals done by Hebert Research), Human Services Policy Center, University of Washington, Seattle, Wa., October 21, 1997, draft, 1, 2, 5.

On the local/national gulf in perceptions of school violence—reflected in the views of both students and principals—see Roper Starch Worldwide, "Teens Talk About Violence in Their Schools and Neighborhoods: A Survey of High School and Junior High/Middle School Students" (commissioned by Rolonda, in association with the Harvard Injury Control Center), November 1994, 5, 15–16; and James W. Boothe et al., "The Violence at Your Door," *Executive Educator,* February 1993, 17–22. The same gulf exists in teens' perceptions of drug use. See Richard Morin and Mario A. Brossard, "Communication Breakdown on Drugs," *Washington Post,* March 4, 1997.

In 1996, a poll of 1,206 registered voters by Princeton Survey Research Associates for Knight-Ridder revealed just how much people's perception of crime hinged on its purported locale. Of those asked "I'd like your views on how much risk there is of becoming a crime victim in some different places," 72 percent said the odds of becoming a victim were "very high" or "high" in the largest city in the state, and 56 percent said the same about the country as a whole. However, just 11 percent thought the risk of becoming a victim was very high or high in their own neighborhood, and only 23 percent thought the risk was high in their city or town. Princeton Survey Research, "Princeton Survey Research, Knight-Ridder Campaign '96 Project, National Survey I," Topline Results, January 17, 1996, 12.

45. Pew Research Center for the People & the Press, "The Optimism Gap Grows," Washington, D.C., news release, January 17, 1997, 3.

46. In 1964, about one in three adults of all ages gave the state of the nation

a high rating. By 1997, only about one in six adults under the age of 63 gave the country a high rating. Pew Research Center for the People & the Press, *Deconstructing Distrust: How Americans View Government* (Washington, D.C.: Pew Research Center for The People & The Press, 1998), 9.

47. Pew Research Center for The People & The Press, "The Optimism Gap Grows," 56–69.

48. David Ellwood, "What to Watch For," *Nieman Reports,* Spring 1997, 27.

49. Susan E. Mayer, *What Money Can't Buy* (Cambridge, Mass.: Harvard University Press, 1997), 23–24.

F. Allan Hanson points out that "until recently, poverty has never been simply the existence of poor people.... During the Middle Ages, poverty was no social pathology but, rather, an instrinsic part of the established social order. Rich and poor alike were said to owe their positions to the grace of God rather than to anything they themselves had done, and all were expected to accept their lot with humility. No stigma was attached to poverty. If anything, the poor were thought to be morally superior to the rich. Monks, nobles, and wealthy people would wash the feet of paupers and invite them to dine.... By the nineteenth century, the prevailing view had been utterly transformed. The poor were despised, instead of honored, and poverty became a social cancer to be eradicated. The idea that the poor were in the image of Christ ended when bad harvests, famine, plague, and runaway inflation—striking at various times from the thirteenth through the sixteenth centuries—produced an army of ragtag paupers who wandered from town to town begging, stealing, and assaulting." F. Allan Hanson, "Why Don't We Care About the Poor Anymore?" *Humanist,* November/December 1997, 11.

50. Diana Mutz, "Impersonal Influence in American Politics," *Public Perspective,* November/December 1992, 19–21.

51. Ronald Inglehart reports that from 1981 to 1990, interpersonal trust rose in 13 of the 21 countries polled in the World Values surveys. The surveys asked people whether they thought "most people can be trusted?" Ronald Inglehart, "Postmaterialist Values and the Erosion of Institutional Authority," in Joseph S. Nye, Jr., Philip D. Zelikow, and David C. King, eds., *Why People Don't Trust Government* (Cambridge, Mass.: Harvard University Press, 1997), 231. However, in the United States, interpersonal trust dropped sharply between 1964 and 1994—in 1964, 54 percent of Americans said most people can be trusted, compared to 35 percent in 1994. *Ibid.,* 231, 216.

52. Hazel Rose Markus and Shinobu Kitayama, "Culture and the Self: Implications for Cognition, Emotion, and Motivation," *Psychological Review,* vol. 98, no. 2 (1991), 223–53; Michael H. Bond et al., "The Social Impact of Self-Effacing Attributions: The Chinese Case," *Journal of Social Psychology,* vol. 118 (1982), 157–66.

53. Alexander W. Astin et al., *The American Freshman: Thirty Year Trends, 1966–1996,* Higher Education Research Institute, University of California at Los Angeles, February 1997, 16, 36. The 1997 freshmen survey, released after the manuscript for *The Optimism Gap* was completed, shows freshmen continue to rate their academic ability, artistic ability, and writing ability at near record levels. New all-time highs were set in 1997 for students' self-ratings of their leadership

ability, public speaking ability, intellectual self-confidence, and social self-confidence. Linda J. Sax et al., *The American Freshman: National Norms for Fall 1997*, Higher Education Research Institute, University of California at Los Angeles, December 1997, 15.

54. Unpublished tabulations of the "self-rating" tables from the 1995 college freshmen survey show that just 2 percent of the freshmen thought the understanding of others was below average, 7 percent said their emotional health was less than average, and 10 percent conceded their leadership abilities were below average. Tabulations provided by William Korn of the Higher Education Research Institute, University of California at Los Angeles.

55. Myers, *Social Psychology*, 153; Martin E. P. Seligman, *Learned Optimism* (New York: Pocket Books, 1991), 107–15.

56. Quoted in Taylor, *Positive Illusions*, 3.

57. Quoted in Myers, *Social Psychology*, 148.

58. Seligman, *Learned Optimism*, 95–106, 141–54, 174–84.

CHAPTER FOUR: The Myth of Social Regression

1. Cited in *Gale's Quotations: Who Said What?* Gale Research, 1995, on CD-ROM.

2. Jill Smolowe, "Ripped from the Womb," *Time*, December 4, 1995, 61.

3. House Speaker Newt Gingrich's Remarks to the Republican Governors Association, Clarion Hotel, Nashua, N.H., November 21, 1995, 4, transcript by the Federal News Service.

4. Jay R. Campbell et al., "Report in Brief: NAEP 1994 Trends in Academic Progress," National Center for Education Statistics, October 1996, table 1, pp. 4, 8.

5. Kevin Gonzalez (spokesperson for Educational Testing Service, Princeton, N.J.), interview with author, April 1997.

6. The 1970 homicide rate comes from Federal Bureau of Investigation, *Crime in the United States, 1975: Uniform Crime Reports*, U.S. Department of Justice, table 1, p. 49; the 1995 homicide figure is in Federal Bureau of Investigation, *Crime in the United States, 1996: Uniform Crime Reports*, U.S. Department of Justice, table 1, p. 62.

7. Ibid. During the 23-year period from 1971 to 1994, the homicide rate was higher every year than in 1995, with the exception of 1984 and 1985.

8. William Hillman, *Mr. President: The First Publication from the Personal Diaries, Private Letters, Papers, and Revealing Interviews of Harry S. Truman* (New York: Farrar, Straus and Young, 1952), 84.

9. Al Gore, *Earth in the Balance* (Boston: Houghton Mifflin, 1992), 49–50.

10. George Mitchell, *World on Fire* (New York: Charles Scribner & Sons, 1991), 21.

11. Todd S. Purdum, "Clinton Plans to Lift Public out of 'Funk,'" *New York Times*, September 24, 1995.

12. "Transcript of President Clinton's State of the Union Message," *Facts on File*, January 26, 1995, 45.

13. Remarks of Senator Bob Dole to the New Hampshire Legislature, Con-

cord, N.H., February 13, 1996, 4, 3, 1. Transcript from Bob Dole for President Campaign.

14. Dole made his gaffe in the October 16, 1996, debate with Clinton. Administration of William J. Clinton, 1996, *Weekly Compilation of Presidential Documents,* vol. 32, no. 41 (Washington, D.C.: U.S. Superintendent of Documents, 1997), 2,085.

15. Louis Uchitelle and N. R. Kleinfield, "On the Battlefields of Business, Millions of Casualties," *New York Times,* March 3, 1996.

16. January 22, 1996, cover, *U.S. News & World Report.*

17. Carl Rowan, *The Coming Race War in America* (Boston, Mass.: Little, Brown, 1996), 39, 3–6.

18. Ibid., 4, vii.

19. Quoted in Arthur Herman, *The Idea of Decline in Western History* (New York: Free Press, 1997), 187.

20. On the living conditions of blacks in 1950 and earlier in the century, see Clair Brown, *American Standards of Living: 1918–1988* (Oxford, England, and Cambridge, Mass.: Blackwell, 1994). In 1935, for example, only 11 percent of blacks had hot running water, inside toilets, and gas or electricity. See pp. 129, 211, and 223.

21. Tony Brown, *Black Lies, White Lies* (New York: William Morrow, 1995), 8; Cornel West, *Race Matters* (New York: Vintage, 1994 ed.), 155, 19 (emphasis in the original).

22. Lisa Fayle Kaplan, "Most Have Close Friends of a Different Color, but Fear Racial Strife," Gannett News Service, January 19, 1997.

23. Herman, *The Idea of Decline,* 7.

24. "Experts Agree: We're Finished," *New York Times Magazine,* January 19, 1997, 13. I do not exaggerate when I say in the opening paragraph of *The Optimism Gap*'s introduction that people now liken America to Rome before the fall. In a May 1998 speech in Sun City West, Arizona, House Speaker, Newt Gingrich, drew on the novels of Colleen McCullough to warn that America, like the one-time Roman republic, was about to collapse. See Frank Bruni, "Gingrich Sees Echo of Ancient Rome in America Today," *New York Times,* May 3, 1998. See also Pat Buchanan," Do declinists have a point?," *Washington Times,* May 18, 1998; and Tony Bouza, *The Decline and Fall of the American Empire* (New York: Plenum Press, 1996).

25. Robert H. Bork, *Slouching Toward Gomorrah: Modern Liberalism and American Decline* (New York: Regan Books, 1996), 2.

26. Robert Hughes, *Culture of Complaint: The Fraying of America* (New York: Oxford University Press, 1993), 4.

27. Samuel P. Huntingdon, *The Clash of Civilizations and the Remaking of World Order* (New York: Simon & Schuster, 1996), 321.

28. Zbigniew Brzezinski, *Out of Control: Global Turmoil on the Eve of the Twenty-first Century* (New York: Charles Scribner's Sons, 1993), 113. Some prominent Democrats have disputed the declinist analysis of Brzezinski and Yale professor Paul Kennedy—who argued in a best-selling book in the late 1980s (*The Rise and Fall of the Great Powers*) that America was ineluctably declining. See Daniel

Patrick Moynihan, "Debunking the Myth of Decline," *New York Times Magazine,* June 19, 1988, 34–36.

29. Edward N. Luttwak, *The Endangered American Dream: How to Stop the United States from Becoming a Third World Country and How to Win the Geo-economic Struggles for Industrial Supremacy* (New York: Simon & Schuster, 1993), 118.

30. Herman, *The Idea of Decline,* 9, 442.

31. Paul R. Ehrlich and Anne H. Ehrlich, *Betrayal of Science and Reason: How Anti-Environmental Rhetoric Threatens Our Future* (Washington, D.C.: Island Press, 1996), 11.

32. Noam Chomsky, "Rollback," in Greg Ruggiero and Stuart Sahulka, eds., *The New American Crisis* (New York: New Press, 1995), 15.

33. Jeremy Rifkin, *The End of Work* (New York: G. P. Putnam's Sons, 1995), 13–14.

34. Charles Lindholm and John A. Hall, "Is the United States Falling Apart?" *Daedalus,* vol. 126, no. 2 (spring 1997), 183–209.

The *Daedalus* article is hardly unprecedented. In its November 1995 issue, *Commentary* questions more than 50 American intellectuals as to whether they agree with the statement "The United States, which in 1945 entered upon the postwar era confident in its democratic purposes and serene in the possession of a common culture, is now, fifty years later, moving toward balkanization or even breakdown." The majority of respondents, most of whom are neoconservatives, agree the United States is headed for a breakdown. William Bennett, for instance, writes that "there is no longer a serious question about whether much of our national project is unraveling. There is, in fact, overwhelming evidence that it is. . . . we have experienced an astonishing degree of social regression" (20). However, a few conservatives dissent. Seymour Martin Lipset concludes, "Is the nation unraveling? The evidence is otherwise" (77); Irving Kristol opines, "I do not for a moment believe that the United States is headed toward balkanization or breakdown, despite all the twaddle about multiculturalism and diversity" (73).

35. The editors, "The End of Democracy? The Judicial Usurpation of Politics," *First Things,* vol. 67 (November 1996), 18–20.

36. Robert H. Bork, "Our Judicial Oligarchy," in ibid., 24.

37. Charles W. Colson, "Kingdoms in Conflict," in ibid., 36–38.

38. William J. Bennett, "The End of Democracy? A Discussion Continued," *First Things,* vol. 69 (January 1997), 19–20.

39. Cheryl Ringel, "Criminal Victimization 1996: Changes 1995–96 with Trends 1993–96," National Crime Victimization Survey, Bureau of Justice Statistics, U.S. Department of Justice, NCJ-165812, November 1997, 1, 8; Michael R. Rand, James P. Lynch, and David Cantor, "Criminal Victimization, 1973–75," National Crime Victimization Survey, Bureau of Justice Statistics, U.S. Department of Justice, NCJ-163069, April 1997, 1–4.

40. Ibid.

41. Franklin E. Zimring and Gordon Hawkins, *Crime Is Not the Problem* (New York: Oxford University Press, 1997), 4–7, 44–47.

42. Federal Bureau of Investigation, *Crime in the United States, 1996: Uni-*

form Crime Reports, U.S. Department of Justice, 1997, table 1, p. 62. Preliminary tallies from the FBI show that the number of homicides in the United States fell an additional 9 percent in 1997.

43. The 1969 homicide rate was 7.3 deaths per 100,000 population. Federal Bureau of Investigation, *Crime in the United States, 1975: Uniform Crime Reports,* U.S. Department of Justice, 1976, table 1, p. 49. For homicide rates earlier in the century, see the charts in F. Landis Mackellar and Machiko Yanagishita, "Homicide in the United States: Who's at Risk?" Population Reference Bureau, Washington, D.C., February 1995, no. 21, 9–10; and Clifford Krauss, "Now, How Low Can Crime Go?" *New York Times,* January 29, 1996; and Rachel L. Jones, "A History of Homicide from 1930s to Today," *Miami Herald,* February 2, 1995.

44. Clifford Krauss, "New York Crime Rate Plummets to Levels Not Seen in 30 years," *New York Times,* December 20, 1996; Fox Butterfield, "Number of Slain Police Officers Is Lowest Since 1960," *New York Times,* January 1, 1997.

45. Matt Lait, "Homicides in L.A. Drop to Lowest Total in 20 Years," *Los Angeles Times,* December 29, 1997.

46. National Center for Health Statistics, *Health, United States, 1995* (Hyattsville, Md.: Public Health Service, 1996), 149; Centers for Disease Control, *Monthly Vital Statistics Report,* vol. 45, no. 3 (September 30, 1996), 48.

47. Mackellar and Yanagishita, "Homicide in the United States," 11.

48. January 17–18, 1996, Yankelovich Partners poll of 800 adults, sponsored by *Time*/CNN, retrieved from Public Opinion Online, Roper Center for Public Opinion Research, University of Connecticut at Storrs.

49. July 29–August 4, 1996, poll of 1,397 registered voters, sponsored by the *Chicago Tribune.* Three in four voters thought violent crime had increased during the previous five years in the nation, and 16 percent said the level of violent crime was about the same. Retrieved from Public Opinion Online, Roper Center for Public Opinion Research, University of Connecticut at Storrs, load date September 3, 1996.

50. Timothy S. Grall, *Our Nation's Housing in 1993,* U.S. Bureau of the Census, Current Housing Reports, H121/95-2 (Washington, D.C.: U.S. Government Printing Office, 1995), table 9, p. 21; U.S. Department of Commerce, Bureau of the Census, *American Housing Survey for the United States in 1993: 20th Anniversary Edition of the AHS,* Current Housing Reports, H150/93, February 1995, table 2-8, p. 52.

51. Ibid., table 5-8, pp. 204–205.

52. Maya Federman and David Levine, "Living Conditions of American Families," Council of Economic Advisors, White House, Washington, D.C., July 19, 1995, table 1C, p. 22.

53. Substance Abuse and Mental Health Services Administration, *Preliminary Results from the 1996 National Household Survey on Drug Abuse,* Public Health Service, U.S. Department of Health and Human Services, p. 1, tables 5A and 5B (pp. 60–61). The 1996 National Household Survey on Drug Abuse interviewed a nationally representative sample of the civilian noninstitutionalized population of more than 18,000 persons, age 12 or older.

54. Table 5, "Long Term Trends in *Thirty-Day* Prevalence of Use of Vari-

ous Drugs for Twelfth Graders," the Monitoring the Future Study, University of Michigan, principal investigator Lloyd D. Johnston. Released December 20, 1997, by the University of Michigan and the Department of Health and Human Services. In 1997, 16,000 high school seniors completed the Monitoring the Future survey, which has been administered annually since 1975.

55. Center on Addiction and Substance Abuse at Columbia University, *National Survey of American Attitudes on Substance Abuse,* polling conducted by Luntz Research Companies, July 1995, 31, 49–50, 63. The 1995 CASA survey sampled 2,000 adults as well as 400 youths, ages 12–17.

56. Ibid., 63, 66, 31–32.

57. Richard Morin and Mario A. Brossard, "Communication Breakdown on Drugs," *Washington Post,* March 4, 1997. The *Washington Post*/ABC News survey interviewed 618 parents of teenagers and 527 teens, ages 12 to 17. A review of 47 national surveys on the war on drugs taken between 1978 and 1997 confirms a dramatic split in Americans' perceptions of the scope of the drug problem nationally versus the scope of drug problems close to home. The review found that more than 80 percent of the public thinks that illegal drug use is a big problem for society, but only 27 percent see it as such in their own community. Even among parents and teens—two demographic groups likely to worry about drugs—there is not much concern at the local level. Just 6 percent of parents of teenagers report that illegal drugs pose "a crisis" in their own neighborhood, though 43 percent think they constitute a crisis in the nation at large. In fact, Americans have repeatedly misjudged the severity of the drug crisis in recent decades, ranking the problem of illegal drugs as more severe when drug use is declining, but ranking the severity of the drug problem as less worrisome when drug use is increasing. One explanation for this anomaly is that people have little personal acquaintance with the problem of drug abuse and depend on news reports for interpreting the drug crisis. More than 80 percent of Americans, for example, say drug abuse has never caused problems in their own families. See Robert J. Blendon and John T. Young, "The Public and the War on Illicit Drugs," *JAMA,* vol. 279, no. 11, March 18, 1998, 828–829.

58. Derek Bok, *The State of the Nation* (Cambridge, Mass.: Harvard University Press, 1996) 59, 57–60. More generally, see Jay R. Campbell et al., Educational Testing Service, "Report in Brief: NAEP 1994 Trends in Academic Progress," National Center for Education Statistics, U.S. Department of Education, October 1996; Council of Economic Advisers, *Economic Report of the President,* together with the *Annual Report of the Council of Economic Advisers* (Washington, D.C.: U.S. Government Printing Office, 1996), 194; David Berliner and Bruce J. Biddle, *The Manufactured Crisis* (Reading, Mass.: Addison-Wesley, 1995), 32–64; and Peter Schrag, "The Near-Myth of Our Failing Schools," *Atlantic Monthly,* October 1997, 72–76.

59. Brian Powell and Lala Carr Steelman, "Bewitched, Bothered, and Bewildering: The Use and Misuse of State SAT and ACT Scores," *Harvard Educational Review,* vol. 66, no. 1 (spring 1996), 38–39.

60. Berliner and Biddle, *The Manufactured Crisis,* 23–24.

61. The College Entrance Examination Board, *College Bound Seniors* (New York, 1993), 10; Berliner and Biddle, *The Manufactured Crisis,* 21–22.

62. Campbell et al., "Report in Brief." The 1996 NAEP results in math and science are summarized in the National Education Goals Panel, *The National Education Goals Report: Building a Nation of Learners, 1997* (Washington, D.C.: U.S. Government Printing Office, 1997), 43–46.

63. Reynolds Farley, *The New American Reality* (New York: Russell Sage Foundation, 1996), 335.

64. Rene Sanchez, "Blacks, Whites Finish High School at Same Rate," *Washington Post,* September 6, 1996. The Census Bureau analyzed black and white dropout rates among 25- to 29-year-olds. In part, the rates by race were close to equivalent because a higher proportion of blacks than whites had initially dropped out of high school but proportionately more blacks had subsequently earned GEDs. But the dropout rate from high school fell between 1975 and 1995 among younger adults, ages 18 to 21, too. U.S. Bureau of the Census, *Statistical Abstract of the United States: 1997* (Washington, D.C.: National Technical Information Service, 1997), 176. Annual dropout rates—that is, how many students dropped out of school in a given grade—also declined between 1973 and 1989 for white and black students. Robert M. Hauser, "Indicators of High School Completion and Dropout," in Robert M. Hauser, Brett V. Brown, and William R. Prosser, eds., *Indicators of Children's Well-Being* (New York: Russell Sage Foundation, 1997), 155–59, 172–73.

65. Stanley M. Elam et al., "The 28th annual Phi Delta Kappa/Gallup Poll of the Public's Attitudes Toward the Public Schools," *Phi Delta Kappan,* vol. 78, no. 1 (September 1996).

66. Mellman-Lazarus-Lake, "AASA Nationwide Survey: Analysis of Findings," January 1994, 9, 16, and unpublished cross-tabulations from Lake Research, Washington, D.C.

67. Aaron Wildavsky, "Doing Better and Feeling Worse: The Political Pathology of Health Policy," in John H. Knowles, ed., *Doing Better and Feeling Worse: Health in the United States* (New York: Norton, 1977), 106.

68. The current life expectancy figure is from Centers for Disease Control, National Center for Health Statistics, "Mortality Patterns—Preliminary Data, United States, 1996," *MMWR,* vol. 26, no. 40 (October 10, 1997), 943; the 1970 figure is in U.S. Bureau of the Census, *Statistical Abstract of the United States: 1997,* 88.

69. John Mueller, "The Rise of the Politically Incorrect One-Handed Economist," January 6, 1977, Department of Political Science at the University of Rochester, paper prepared for the Festschrift in Honor of Richard Rosecrance, Palm Springs, Calif., January 24–26, 1997, 14.

70. Bernard Guyer et al., "Annual Summary of Vital Statistics—1996," *Pediatrics,* vol. 100, no. 6 (December 1997), 905.

71. Ibid., 912. Farley, *The New American Reality,* 335.

72. Arlene Holen, "The History of Accident Rates in the United States," in Julian L. Simon, ed., *The State of Humanity* (Oxford, England, and Cambridge, Mass.: Blackwell, 1995), 98–105.

73. Allen M. Brandt, "World Trends in Smoking," in ibid., 107; U.S. Bureau of the Census, *Statistical Abstract of the United States: 1997,* 145.

74. Susan E. Mayer and Christopher Jencks, "Has Poverty Really Increased Among Children Since 1970?" Center for Urban Affairs and Policy Research, Northwestern University, WP-94-14, 1995, table 8.

75. Edward Tenner, *Why Things Bite Back* (New York: Knopf, 1996), 254–55.

76. U.S. Bureau of the Census, Current Population Reports, P60-197, *Money Income in the United States: 1996* (Washington, D.C.: U.S. Government Printing Office, 1997), table B-4, p. B-10.

77. The poverty rate for blacks in 1996 was 28.4 percent, the lowest level since the Census Bureau began formally collecting poverty data in 1959. Before 1959 the poverty rate of blacks was much higher than it has been in the post-1960 era. Leatha Lamison-White, U.S. Bureau of the Census, Current Population Reports, Series P60-198, *Poverty in the United States: 1996* (Washington, D.C.: U.S. Government Printing Office, 1997), vi, C-11, C-12.

78. Stephanie J. Ventura et al., "Births and Deaths: United States, 1996," *Monthly Vital Statistics Report,* Centers for Disease Control, National Center for Health Statistics, vol. 46, no. 1, supplement 2, September 11, 1997, 1.

79. Claudette E. Bennett, U.S. Bureau of the Census, Current Population Reports, P20-480, *The Black Population in the United States: March 1994 and 1993* (Washington, D.C.: U.S. Government Printing Office, 1995), table 1; Current Population Reports, Special Studies Series P-23, no. 80, *The Social and Economic Status of the Black Population in the United States: An Historical View, 1790–1978* (Washington, D.C.: U.S. Government Printing Office, 1980), table 71.

80. Orlando Patterson, *The Ordeal of Integration* (Washington, D.C.: Civitas Counterpoint, 1997), 21. More generally, see Patterson's discussion of the educational progress of blacks, 20–27.

81. Orlando Patterson, "The Paradox of Integration," *New Republic,* November 6, 1995, 26.

82. Howard Schuman, Charlotte Steeh, and Lawrence Bobo, *Racial Attitudes in America* (Cambridge, Mass.: Harvard University Press, 1985), 74–76; *The Gallup Poll Social Audit on Black/White Relations in the United States* (Princeton, N.J.: Gallup Organization, 1997), 59–70. The Gallup poll questioned just over 3,000 adults in January and February 1997, including an oversample of 1,269 black respondents.

83. Douglas J. Besharov and Timothy S. Sullivan, "One Flesh: America Is Experiencing an Unprecedented Increase in Black-White Intermarriage," *New Democrat,* July/August 1996, 19–20. For evidence on the increase in black-white social contact since the 1960s—that is, evidence of more blacks and whites who have interracial friendships, neighbors of another race, dinner guests of another race, interracial church congregations, and so on—see Stephan Thernstrom and Abigail Thernstrom, *America in Black and White: One Nation, Indivisible* (New York: Simon & Schuster, 1997), 520–27. The next generation of black and white adults, now in their teens, are also more integrated in interracial social settings and personally less affected by the prospect of prejudice than their parents. Christopher John Farley, "Kids and Race," *Time,* November 24, 1997, 88–91.

84. *The Gallup Poll Social Audit,* 20–21.

85. "The National Prospect: A Symposium," *Commentary,* November 1995, 23.

86. Schuman, Steeh, and Bobo, *Racial Attitudes in America,* 118–19, 125; Thernstrom and Thernstrom, *America in Black and White,* 102–4, 138–42; Richard Morin, "The Ugly Way We Were," *Washington Post* ("Unconventional Wisdom" column), April 6, 1997.

87. "Gallup Short Subjects," *Gallup Poll Monthly,* July 1996, 42.

88. *The Gallup Poll Social Audit,* 71–72.

The I'm OK–They're Not syndrome also colors blacks' views of racial discrimination. Roughly 60 percent of African-Americans report in surveys that they have not personally experienced discrimination, and roughly three in four say they are satisfied with their standard of living and quality of life. Nevertheless, most African-Americans also think that discrimination against blacks is omnipresent, and only a third believe that the quality of life for blacks in general has improved during the last 10 years. *The Gallup Poll Social Audit,* 22, 10; Lee Sigelman and Susan Welch, *Black Americans' Views of Racial Inequality: The Dream Deferred* (New York: Cambridge University Press, 1991), 59–60.

Ironically, advances in race relations have provided the least solace to those they most benefited—middle-class blacks. Survey after survey shows that middle-class blacks, as political scientist Jennifer Hochschild puts it, are "succeeding more and enjoying it less." Middle-class blacks are more likely than poor blacks to think that discrimination is blacks' most important problem, expect less improvement in race relations in the future, and see less decline in discrimination. Jennifer L. Hochschild, *Facing Up to the American Dream* (Princeton, N.J.: Princeton University Press, 1995), 72–88, 106.

One little-appreciated consequence of the I'm OK–They're Not syndrome is that it deters blacks and whites from trying to move into racially integrated neighborhoods. Blacks who are persuaded that the world is rife with discrimination—even if they themselves have not confronted much of it—may avoid moving into integrated neighborhoods because they believe they will encounter racial hostility there. In effect, their optimism gap becomes a self-fulfilling prophecy: They believe white neighbors would discriminate against them, and by failing to look for housing in white neighborhoods, their convictions remain unchallenged and untested.

In a 1992 survey of 750 blacks in the Detroit area, only about 20 percent said they had actually experienced housing discrimination themselves, yet most blacks also believed that housing discrimination against blacks was rampant in the area. However, those who said they *had* personally faced housing discrimination were actually *more* likely to press ahead to integrate all-white neighborhoods than blacks who said they had not encountered housing discrimination. Reynolds Farley, Charlotte Steeh, Tara Jackson, et al., "Continued Racial Residential Segregation in Detroit: 'Chocolate City, Vanilla Suburbs' Revisited," *Journal of Housing Research,* vol. 4, no. 1, 1993, 18.

Blacks' disabling attitudes are mirrored by whites' I'm OK–They're Not beliefs. The 1992 Detroit poll surveyed about 800 whites as well, the vast majority of whom felt that they weren't prejudiced and that housing discrimination against blacks was on the wane. "Segregated housing patterns currently observed in the Detroit area result in part from the perceptions of blacks and whites about discrimination," the study's authors conclude. "Blacks who can afford homes in the suburban ring may be less likely to seek housing there, since they believe they will face hostility and discrimination in many locations and be unfairly treated by brokers and lenders. Whites may be unwilling to support policies to reduce discrimination, since they see the issue primarily as one of individual whites who are prejudiced. This perceptual gap helps maintain the status quo of residential segregation." Farley et al., "Continued Racial Residential Segregation in Detroit," 20.

The gap that Farley found in his survey research was the same gap that White House aides and members of President Clinton's Advisory Board on Race Relations encountered when they sought during 1997 to promote racial reconciliation. Most of those who testified before the advisory board believed that racism was a serious, enduring problem. But relatively few suggested that they themselves or people they knew were part of the problem. Jonathan Coleman, author of the 1997 book *Long Way to Go* (a study of race problems in Milwaukee), was among those consulted by the White House. Coleman had just returned from a 20-city book tour and was struck by the "cynicism around the whole question of race. Many people were incredulous—especially whites. They wondered how I could spend so much time on a problem that they at once felt was insolvable and one that they did not believe much affected their lives." Quoted in Michael A. Fletcher and Peter Baker, "Clinton Sees Today's Town Hall Meeting as Turning Point in His Race Initiative," *Washington Post*, December 3, 1997.

One paradox of the Detroit study—that is, those most likely to personally encounter discrimination were also those might likely to end up living in integrated neighborhoods—has popped up elsewhere in the country. Orlando Patterson has pointed out that blacks who confront racial harassment from whites when moving to the suburbs nonetheless often end up building strong relations with other white neighbors. This was one of the "surprise" findings of the famed Gautreaux project, which subsidized the move of hundreds of low-income black residents of Chicago's housing projects to the suburbs and other neighborhoods. (Patterson, *The Ordeal of Integration*, 54)

Of course, neither Patterson, Jackson, nor anyone else is claiming that housing discrimination is imaginary, or that discrimination is not a prime reason why housing segregation persists. But the perceptions and misperceptions of race matter, too—and rarely receive any attention from the media in stories on segregation.

89. Transcript of President William J. Clinton's remarks at a February 15, 1996, presidential fund-raising gala at the Sheraton Imperial Ballroom, New York, N.Y. Federal Document Clearing House, 4.

90. Humphrey Taylor, chairman of the Harris poll, has also pointed out that public opinion about America remains glum precisely because most Americans don't believe social conditions have improved. Humphrey Taylor, "Why Is Public Opinion So Gloomy? Because Most People Don't Know Crime Is Declining, or That Economy and Jobs Are Growing," Harris poll 1996, no. 31, Louis Harris and Associates, New York, released May 20, 1996, 1–5. The 1996 Harris

poll found that 81 percent of the public mistakenly thought violent crime was increasing in the country (63 percent thought it was "increasing a lot"), and only a third of respondents knew the economy was growing and adding jobs.

91. In the 1950s, most Americans didn't think they were living in the good ol' days either. People complained regularly about the spiritual bankruptcy of the day, wayward youths, how unprecedented affluence was corrupting Americans, and other woes that would feel very familiar today. The social philosopher Albert Schweitzer, sounding suspiciously like Newt Gingrich, opened a 1950 book with the observation: "We are living today under the sign of the collapse of civilization. . . . the ethical ideas on which civilization was built have been wandering about the world, poverty-stricken and helpless. . . . We have lost ourselves in outward progress. . . . [We have allowed] all advance in the moral life to come to a stand-still." Quoted in Herman, *The Idea of Decline*, 291.

For other references on American dissatisfaction in the 1950s, see Jeff Greenfield, "Voter Anxiety: A Chronic Condition," *Time*, April 22, 1996, 58; Stephanie Coontz, *The Way We Never Were: American Families and the Nostalgia Trap* (New York: Basic Books, 1992); and Mike A. Males, *The Scapegoat Generation* (Monroe, Maine: Common Courage Press, 1996).

CHAPTER FIVE: The Myth of Moral Decline

1. Charles Dickens, *Martin Chuzzlewit* (1844), chap. 16.

2. Quoted in Arthur Herman, *The Idea of Decline in Western History* (New York: Free Press, 1997), 285.

3. Al Gore, *Earth in the Balance* (Boston: Houghton Mifflin, 1992), 367.

4. In a 1996 *Wall Street Journal* poll, 61 percent of the public said the state of morals in America was "pretty bad and getting worse," compared to 41 percent who gave the same answer in 1964. Ellen Graham and Cynthia Crossen, "God, Motherhood, and Apple Pie," *Wall Street Journal*, December 13, 1996 (American Opinion section). Seymour Martin Lipset provides some historical comparisons in *American Exceptionalism* (New York: Norton, 1996), 267.

5. According to a 1996 Gallup Organization survey (sponsored by the Church of Jesus Christ of Latter-Day Saints), 76 percent of adults think the country's moral direction is worse than when they were children. The Gallup Organization, Princeton, N.J., November 1996 fieldwork, cross-tabulations, 144. An April 1997 survey of 900 adults by Luntz Research Companies for the Christian Coalition found that 80 percent agreed there was a "moral crisis in America today." Cheryl Wetzstein, "Poll Finds Growing Concern over 'Moral Direction,' " *Washington Times*, April 23, 1997.

6. John Fantuzzo et al., Domestic Violence and Children: Prevalence and Risk in Five Major U.S. Cities," *Journal of American Academy of Child Adolescent Psychiatry*, vol. 36, no. 1 (January 1997), 116–22; Robert Whelan, *Broken Homes and Battered Children: A Study of the Relationship Between Child Abuse and Family Type* (London: Family Education Trust Fund, 1993).

7. Andrea Sedlak and Diane D. Broadhurst, *The Third National Incidence Study of Child Abuse and Neglect*, prepared by Westat for the U.S. Department of Health and Human Services, September 1996.

8. See the online exchange in *Slate* between Douglas Besharov, "Child Abuse: Threat or Menace? How Common Is It Really?" (posted October 3, 1996), and Andrea Sedlak and Diana Broadhurst's response, "Fact Abuse" (posted October 23, 1996). Besharov's subsequent reply was posted the same day.

9. Michaels Opinion Research, "American Family Values: Seventh National Survey," New York, October 1995 (sponsored by the Massachusetts Mutual Life Insurance Company), 4. A 1997 poll sponsored by the *Washington Post,* the Henry J. Kaiser Family Foundation, and Harvard University confirms that Americans think they have great marriages. Sixty-six percent of husbands and wives surveyed felt their marriage was either "perfect and couldn't be improved" or "it's nearly perfect; a few small improvements are needed." By contrast, just 4 percent of the spouses said their marriage was not so good or was in real trouble. Claudia Deane, "Husbands and Wives," *Washington Post,* March 24, 1998.

10. The Pew Research Center for the People & the Press, "Motherhood Today—A Tougher Job, Less Ably Done," Washington, D.C., news release, May 9, 1997, 20.

Teenagers evidence the same I'm OK–They're Not mind-set as their parents. They believe drugs, peer pressure, and AIDS are the major problems confronting teens in general, but their biggest personal problems are the same ones that have plagued teens for decades: their grades, their college prospects, and their appearance. Richard G. Braungart and Margaret M. Braungart, "Today's Youth, Tomorrow's Citizens," *Public Perspective,* August/September 1995, 4–7; Richard G. Braungart and Margaret M. Braungart, "Youth Violence, Citizenship, and Citizenship Education in the United States in the 1990s," forthcoming in Meredith Watts, ed., *Cross-Cultural Perspectives on Youth, Radicalism, and Violence* (Greenwich, Conn.: JAI Press, 1998).

Despite all the lamentations about "kids today," today's youths, on most measures, are actually better off than their parents were a quarter century ago. They are less likely to smoke, drink, or do drugs, less likely to drive drunk or die from a drug overdose, and more likely to finish high school and college. Not every social ill afflicting youth has diminished, but most have. David Whitman, "The Youth 'Crisis,' " *U.S. News & World Report,* May 5, 1997, 24–27; Mike A. Males, *The Scapegoat Generation: America's War on Adolescents* (Monroe, Maine: Common Courage Press, 1996).

11. For data on parents' belief that they are better parents than their own parents, see the references in note 29, chap. 1.

Survey data comparing the values of today's parents with parents in 1976–77 appears in "The American Character," *Wall Street Journal* (American Opinion section), March 5, 1998. The *Journal's* 1998 poll showed that the percentage of parents who rated hard work, having children, patriotism, and religion as being "very important" rose roughly 20 to 30 points in the last two decades.

Gallup polls dating back to the early 1950s show virtually no change over the last half-century in parents' willingness to spank children, in their support of having primary-school-age children stand up when older guests enter a room, and in their practice of saying grace aloud before meals. The Gallup polls also show that parents give themselves high marks for their childrearing skills. In 1997, only

2 percent of parents gave themselves a grade of a "D" for the job they were doing bringing up their kids, yet most Americans did not think that parents generally do a good job preparing children for the future. Frank Newport, "Americans' Relationship With Their Children: Much Remains the Same," *Gallup Poll Monthly,* March 1997, 13–16, 44–50.

12. Michaels Opinion Research, "National Public Opinion Survey: Commitment and American Society," New York, November 1994 (sponsored by the Massachusetts Mutual Life Insurance Company), 5, 12, 23, unnumbered pages from chap. 2 (reproducing questionnaire results).

13. Michaels Opinion Research, "American Family Values," 15–16, appendix A, vi, viii.

14. David Whitman, "The Divorce Dilemma," *U.S. News & World Report,* September 30, 1996, 58–60. Much publicized efforts by state legislators and governors to reform no-fault divorce laws in Michigan and Iowa in 1996 died in the legislatures. The only state that altered its no-fault law in a fundamental way was Louisiana. Kevin Sack, "Louisiana Approves Measure to Tighten Marriage Bonds," *New York Times,* June 24, 1997. The Louisiana law gave couples the option of obtaining a "covenant marriage" license. This special license was meant to curb couples' right to a no-fault divorce—they could divorce only in cases where the traditional "fault" grounds existed, such as a spouse who had committed adultery, was abusive, or was imprisoned for a felony. The response to the Louisiana law has been meager. Six months after it took effect, only 120 covenant marriage licenses have been issued. Family Relations, *State Capitals Newsletters,* March 9, 1998, 4.

15. David Kirkpatrick, "What Kind of Impact Do You Feel These Social Movements Have Had on Today's Values?" *Wall Street Journal,* December 13, 1996 (American Opinion section). The *Journal* polled 2,003 respondents.

16. James Davison Hunter and Carl Bowman, *The State of Disunion: 1996 Survey of American Political Culture,* vol. 2, the Post-Modernity Project, University of Virginia (In Medias Res Educational Foundation, Ivy, Va.), tables 6.B through 6.H.

17. Paul Starobin, "Politics of the Past," *National Journal,* February 17, 1997, 354–58; Steven Thomma, "Nostalgia for '50s Surfaces in Survey," *Philadelphia Inquirer,* February 4, 1996; Princeton Survey Research, "Princeton Survey Research, Knight-Ridder Campaign '96 Project, National Survey I," Topline Results, January 17, 1996, 2.

18. In an August 1994 poll for *Newsweek* of 750 adults, Princeton Survey Research Associates found that 75 percent of the respondents believed "the United States is in a moral and spiritual decline." Retrieved from Public Opinion Online, Roper Center for Public Opinion Research, University of Connecticut at Storrs, load date January 1, 1995. See also the Gallup Organization, Princeton, N.J., November 1996 fieldwork, cross-tabulations, 144. Just 6 percent of respondents in the Gallup survey thought the country's moral direction was better today than when they were children.

19. Lipset, *American Exceptionalism,* 62, 275.

20. The Tarrance Group and Mellman, Lazarus & Lake, marginals from a

poll of 1,045 registered voters, March 5–7, 1994, conducted for *U.S. News & World Report.*

21. Russell Short, "Belief by the Numbers," *New York Times Magazine,* December 7, 1997, 60.

22. Frank Newport and Lydia Saad, "Religious Faith Is Widespread But Many Skip Church," *Gallup Poll Monthly,* March 1997, 20–21.

23. Ibid; Short, "Belief by the Numbers," 60.

24. Newport and Saad, "Religious Faith Is," 23.

25. Short, "Belief by the Numbers," 60; Karlyn Bowman, "Poll-Pouri," *Women's Quarterly,* vol. 11 (spring 1997), 27.

26. George Gallup, Jr., "Religion in America—Will the Vitality of Churches Be the Surprise of the Next Century?" *Public Perspective,* October/November 1995, 3, 4.

27. Roger Finke and Rodney Stark, *The Churching of America, 1776–1990* (New Brunswick, N.J.: Rutgers University Press, 1992), 7; Richard Morin, "The Way We Weren't: Religion in Colonial America," *Washington Post* ("Unconventional Wisdom" column), November 26, 1995.

28. Everett Carll Ladd, "The Myth of Moral Decline," *Responsive Community,* winter 1993–94, 52–68. Ladd discusses earlier polls at 52–53.

29. Lipset, *American Exceptionalism,* 267.

30. Ann E. Kaplan, ed., AAFRC Trust for Philanthropy, *Giving USA, 1995: The Annual Report on Philanthropy for the Year 1994* (New York: American Association of Fund-Raising Counsel, 1995), 48: earlier data in AAFRC Trust for Philanthropy, *Giving USA, 1985: Estimates of Philanthropic Giving in 1985 and the Trends They Show* (New York: American Association of Fund-Raising Counsel, 1986), 10, data sheet 1; Ladd, "The Myth of Moral Decline," 65; "Charitable Giving Has Continued to Rise Sharply and Steadily," *Public Perspective,* June/July 1996, 17.

31. In 1991, 41 percent of Americans were involved in charitable activities such as helping the poor, the sick, or the elderly. Ladd, "The Myth of Moral Decline," 65; by 1994, the figure had risen to 48 percent. Lipset, *American Exceptionalism,* 277. In 1997, the percentage of college freshmen—73.1 percent—who said they did volunteer work in the year prior to college was higher than at any time since the college freshmen survey first inquired about volunteer activities, in 1984. Linda J. Sax et al., *The American Freshman: National Norms for Fall 1997,* Higher Education Research Institute, Graduate School of Education and Information Studies, University of California at Los Angeles, December 1997, 15.

32. Research Division, Internal Revenue Service, *Income Tax Compliance Research: Net Tax Gap and Remittance Gap Estimates (Supplement to Publication 7285),* Department of the Treasury, IRS Publication 1415 (4-90), 1–2.

33. Ladd, "The Myth of Moral Decline," 61–62.

34. Fred Schab, "Schooling Without Learning: Thirty Years of Cheating in High School," *Adolescence,* vol. 26, no. 104 (winter 1991), 839–47.

35. Donald L. McCabe and Linda Klebe Trevino, "What We Know About Cheating in College: Longitudinal Trends and Recent Developments," *Change,* January/February 1996, 29–33.

36. Ladd, "The Myth of Moral Decline," 57.

37. Robert D. Putnam, "Bowling Alone: America's Declining Social Capital," *Journal of Democracy,* vol. 6, no. 1 (January 1995), 65–78. Subsequently Putnam elaborated on the notion of civic decline in "Tuning In, Tuning Out: The Strange Disappearance of Social Capital in America," *P.S.: Political Science and Politics,* December 1995, 664–82.

38. Robert Samuelson, "Harvard Scholar Misses the Point of 'Real Life,' " *Chicago Tribune,* April 12, 1996; Nicholas Lemann, "Kicking in Groups," *Atlantic Monthly,* April 1996, 22–26; Everett C. Ladd, "The Data Just Don't Show Erosion of America's 'Social Capital,' " opening to special section of *Public Perspective,* June/July 1996, 1–49; Michael Schudson, "What If Civic Life Didn't Die?" *American Prospect,* no. 25 (March/April 1996), 17–20; John Clark, "Shifting Engagements: Lessons from the 'Bowling Alone' Debate," Hudson Briefing Paper, no. 196, October 1996, Hudson Institute, Indianapolis, Ind., 1–16; Richard Stengel, "Bowling Together," *Time,* July 22, 1996, 35–36; and Peter Y. Hong, "Bowling Alley Tour Refutes Theory of Social Decline," *Los Angeles Times,* March 18, 1996. Participating in a bowling league may not be the clearest proof of wholesome civic commitment—Oklahoma city bombers Timothy McVeigh and Terry Nichols were in a bowling league, too.

39. John P. Robinson and Geoffrey Godbey, *Time for Life: The Surprising Ways Americans Use Their Time* (University Park, Pa.: Pennsylvania State University Press, 1997), 176.

CHAPTER SIX: The Myth of Economic Decline

1. Quoted in John Mueller, "The Rise of the Politically Incorrect One-Handed Economist," January 6, 1977, Department of Political Science at the University of Rochester, paper prepared for the Festschrift in Honor of Richard Rosecrance, Palm Springs, Calif., January 24–26, 1997, 13.

2. "Transcript of President Clinton's State of the Union Message," *Facts on File,* January 26, 1995, 47.

3. Forty-seven percent of voters thought the economy was in a recession in October 1995 (53 percent thought so in October 1994). "The Mood of America," *Los Angeles Times,* November 5, 1995. (The wording of the poll question was "On another subject, do you think we are in an economic recession, or not?") The *Times* poll interviewed 1,426 adults nationwide, including 1,190 registered voters. *Los Angeles Times Poll,* Study 369, October 1995, National Survey, 1, 3.

A January 1996 poll for *U.S. News & World Report* found that just 22 percent of the public believed the economy was expanding. Another 37 percent thought the economy was stagnating, and 20 percent thought the country was in a recession. A staggering 11 percent—or one in nine Americans—felt the economy was in a depression. Steven V. Roberts, "Workers Take It on the Chin," *U.S. News & World Report,* January 22, 1996, 44.

4. ABC News/*Money* Consumer Index, "Consumer Confidence Soars to New Heights," December 4, 1996, America Online: UsnewsA, 4; David Whitman, "Things Are Getting Better? Who Knew?" *U.S. News & World Report,* December 16, 1996, 30–32.

5. Lynn A. Karoly of the Rand Institute summarizes the growth in inequality from 1973 to 1993 in "Anatomy of the U.S. Income Distribution: Two Decades of Change," *Oxford Review of Economic Policy*, vol. 12, no. 1 (1996), 77–95, as does Sheldon Danziger and Peter Gottschalk in *America Unequal* (Cambridge, Mass.: Harvard University Press and the Russell Sage Foundation, 1995). The 1998 annual report of the Council of Economic Advisers updates the time-series on real hourly earnings to 1997 and provides more recent numbers on income inequality. *Economic Report of the President*, transmitted to Congress February 1998 (Washington, D.C., U.S. Government Printing Office, 1998), 125–150; 336. Herbert Stein and Murray Foss of the American Enterprise Institute chart the Census Bureau data on median family income from 1973 to 1992 in *The New Illustrated Guide to the American Economy*, 2nd ed. (Washington, D.C.: AEI Press, 1995), 102–5.

Until recently it appeared that the distribution of wealth (as well as the distribution of income) had become much more unequal in the United States during the last two decades. Edward N. Wolff, *Top Heavy: A Study of the Increasing Inequality of Wealth in America* (New York: Twentieth Century Fund Press, 1995). But more recent data from the Federal Reserve Board's 1992 and 1995 Survey of Consumer Finances indicate that both median family net wealth, and the concentration of wealth in the top 10th and richest 2 percent of families, were about the same in 1992 as in 1983. The distribution of wealth has probably become slightly more equal since then. *Economic Report of the President*, 182–83; Arthur B. Kennickell, Douglas A. McManus, and R. Louis Woodburn, "Weighting Design for the 1992 Survey of Consumer Finances," March 1996, 18, 23, 26; Steven Pearlstein, "The Rich Are Getting Richer; So Is the Working Class," *Washington Post*, January 23, 1997; John C. Weicher, "Increasing Inequality of Wealth?" *Public Interest*, winter 1997, 15–25.

6. Family size declined from 2.8 persons in 1973 to 2.4 persons in 1992. Stein and Foss, *The New Illustrated Guide*, 104. See also Robert J. Samuelson, "The Typical Household Isn't," *Washington Post*, October 8, 1997.

7. Stein and Foss, *The New Illustrated Guide*, 102–3.

8. Committee on Ways and Means, U.S. House of Representatives, *1996 Green Book*, Ways and Means Committee Print 104–14, November 4, 1996 (Washington, D.C.: U.S. Government Printing Office, 1996), 1,031.

9. Advisory Commission to Study the Consumer Price Index, "Toward a More Accurate Measure of the Cost of Living," final report to the Senate Finance Committee, December 4, 1996; Steven Pearlstein, "Head of Statistics Bureau Balks at Plan to Alter CPI: Abraham Doubts Inflation Overstated by 1.1%," *Washington Post*, December 20, 1996.

10. Michael J. Boskin, "Prisoner of Faulty Statistics," American Enterprise Institute for Public Policy Research, Washington, D.C., January 1997, 1–2 (a shorter version of Boskin's article appeared in the *Wall Street Journal*, December 5, 1996).

11. Calculated from background tables for Stein and Foss, *The New Illustrated Guide*, 102–5.

12. Robert J. Samuelson, "The Two-Earner Myth," *Washington Post*, January 22, 1997. Chinhui Juhn, a professor of economics at the University at Houston,

has pointed out that the increase in work among married women has been mainly concentrated among the spouses of high-wage-earning husbands, not among women married to husbands with low wages. For men in the lowest decile (i.e., the bottom tenth), the employment rate of wives increased by about 15 percentage points from 1969 to 1989. But it increased 35 percentage points for wives in the top decile. In 1969, women whose husbands' wages were at the low end of the wage distribution were more likely to work than other women. By 1989, they were less likely to be working than women married to middle-class earners (and they were no more likely to be working than women married to high-wage earners). "Relative wage Trends, Women's Work, and Family Income," American Enterprise Institute for Public Policy Research, Washington, D.C., Conference Summary, January 1997, 1–2.

13. "Women and Work," *American Enterprise,* March/April 1996, 91; Cathy Young, "What Do Women Really Want?" *Philadelphia Inquirer,* November 9, 1996.

14. The 1997 poll results of working women's attitudes are cited in "Changes and Gender Roles," *Washington Post,* March 22, 1998. According to the *Post*/Henry J. Kaiser Family Foundation/Harvard University poll, 30 percent of employed women said they would work the same amount even if they could do just as well without working, 52 percent said they would work fewer hours or days per week, and 17 percent said they would stop working altogether. Susan Chira provides a helpful summary of women's conflicted attitudes toward work in *A Mother's Place* (New York: HarperCollins, 1998), 149–154.

Studies showing that working mothers are more satisfied than nonworking mothers are summarized in Lois Wladis Hoffman, "Effects of Maternal Employment in the Two-Parent Family," *American Psychologist,* vol. 44, no. 2, February 1989, 283–292; and Rosalind C. Barnett and Caryl Rivers, *He Works, She Works* (New York: HarperCollins, 1996).

15. *Economic Report to the President,* 317. For 1997, the Council of Economic Advisers reported quarterly readings on both Americans' personal per capita disposable income and on their personal consumption expenditures. To be conservative about the growth in disposable income and consumption, I have used the lowest quarterly figures from 1997. If the highest figures, from the last quarter of 1997, were the basis of comparison, the real increase in disposable income and consumption since 1973 would go up an additional 3 percentage points or so.

It is worth noting a downside to people's burgeoning spending—Americans save less today than at any time since the Depression.

16. Ibid.

17. Cited in Mike Glover, Associated Press, "Buchanan Hits Dole over Trade," *Philadelphia Inquirer,* February 29, 1996.

18. Lawrence Mishel and Jared Bernstein, *The State of Working America, 1994–95,* Economic Policy Institute Series (Armonk, N.Y.: M. E. Sharpe, 1994), 121.

19. Ibid., 74.

20. Peter Gottschalk's review of studies of income mobility shows there is no evidence that mobility has increased. Peter Gottschalk, "Notes on 'By Our

Own Bootstraps: Economic Opportunity and the Dynamics of Income' by Cox and Alm," April 22, 1996, unpublished paper, Boston College, Economics Department, 1–6. Several of Gottschalk's tables are reprinted in Lawrence Mishel, Jared Bernstein, and John Schmitt, The State of Working America, 1996–97 (Washington, D.C., Economic Policy Institute, 1996), 95–97. Daniel McMurrer and Isabel Sawhill also conclude that "mobility has not changed significantly over the last 25 years," in "How Much Do Americans Move Up and Down the Economic Ladder?" Urban Institute, Opportunity in America Series, no. 3, September 1996, 2. Finally, Syracuse economics professor Douglas Holtz-Eakin and his colleagues have also compared mobility rates during the 1970s and 1980s and found little change. Letter from Douglas Holtz-Eakin to author, March 5, 1996.

21. Mishel and Bernstein, The State of Working America, 1994–95, 74.

22. Gottschalk, "Notes on 'By Our Own Bootstraps,'" 3.

23. Daniel P. McMurrer and Isabel V. Sawhill, "The Declining Importance of Class," Urban Institute, Opportunity in America Series, no. 4, April 1997, 2; Daniel P. McMurrer, Mark Condon, and Isabel V. Sawhill, "Intergenerational Mobility in the United States," Urban Institute, May 1997, 18, 23, 24.

24. John Sabelhaus and Joyce Manchester, "Baby Boomers and Their Parents: How Does Their Economic Well-Being Compare in Middle Age?" Journal of Human Resources, vol. 30, no. 4 (fall 1995), 791–806.

25. U.S. Department of Housing and Urban Development, "Homeownership Rate Hits 66%—Highest Level in America's History Bringing Homeownership to a Record 67.6 Million Families," HUD news Release no. 97-228, October 23, 1997, 1–3. According to the decennial census, the home ownership rate in the "good ol' days"—when homes were allegedly affordable—was 61.9 percent in 1960 and 62.9 percent in 1970.

26. Married couples under the age of 45, and people as a whole under that age, were less likely to own their own home in 1996 than in 1982. Those 45 and over were more likely to own their home in 1996 than in 1982. "Table 15: Homeownership Rates for the United States by Age of Householder and by Family Status," Current Population Survey, U.S. Bureau of the Census. The home ownership rates by age are unpublished but available on the Internet at http://wwww.census.gov/hhes/www/hvs.html.

27. W. Michael Cox and Richard Alm, "Time Well Spent: The Declining Real Cost of Living in America," 1997 Annual Report of the Federal Reserve Bank of Dallas, 1998, 8.

28. Ibid., 2–24. Cox and Alm concluded that the median number of hours a homeowner worked to pay for each square foot of a new house rose 10 percent from 1970 to 1996. However, families today are smaller than they were in 1970. When Cox and Alm adjust their figures to reflect the fact that families are now smaller, the typical individual's housing cost was actually 6 percent cheaper in 1996 than in 1970.

29. Paul Krugman, "It's a Wonderful Life," Washington Monthly, January/February 1996, 49.

30. Jeff Pelline, "America's Love Affair with PC's Heating Up: Sales of Computers Surpass Color TVs," San Francisco Chronicle, January 6, 1995.

31. From the Consumer Electronics Manufacturers Association, cited in "The Technology Culture," *Wall Street*, June 16, 1997 (Technology section).

A number of journalists have carefully documented the rise in living standards since the 1970s. See Paul Richter, "It Just Seems Like We're Worse Off," *Los Angeles Times*, January 26, 1995; David Wessel and Bob Davis, "In the Middle of the Middle: Two Families' Stories," *Wall Street Journal*, March 29, 1995; and W. Michael Cox and Rick Alm, "The Good Old Days Are Now," *Reason*, December 1995, 20–27. (Michael Cox is vice president of the Federal Reserve Bank of Dallas.)

32. Associated Press, "A Study Finds Progress in Linking Public Schools to the Internet," *New York Times*, February 18, 1996.

33. Alexander W. Astin et al., *The American Freshman: Thirty Year Trends*, Higher Education Research Institute, Graduate School of Education and Information Studies, University of California at Los Angeles, February 1997, 45.

34. Bruce Felton, "Technologies That Enable the Disabled," *New York Times*, September 14, 1997; Kathi Wolfe, "Enabling the Disabled: Where There's a Wheel, There's a Way," *Hemisphere*, June 1997, 123–25.

35. Unpublished data from the U.S. decennial census, provided by Professor Christopher Jencks, John F. Kennedy School of Government, Harvard University.

36. Ibid.

The percentage of households with children that have two or more automobiles can also be calculated as follows: See Susan E. Mayer and Christopher Jencks, "Has Poverty Really Increased Among Children Since 1970?" Center for Urban Affairs and Policy Research, Northwestern University, Working Paper 94-14, 1995, table 7; add the mean for each quintile of households listed in the table and then divide the sum by five.

37. Unpublished data from the 1973 and 1995 American Housing Surveys, U.S. Bureau Census, data runs by Joe Swingle, research assistant to Christopher Jencks, John F. Kennedy School of Government, Harvard University.

38. U.S. Bureau of the Census, *Statistical Abstract of the United States: 1974* (Washington, D.C.: U.S. Government Printing Office, 1974), 213; U.S. Bureau of the Census, *Statistical Abstract of the United States: 1995* (Washington, D.C.: U.S. Government Printing Office, 1995), 265.

39. Everett Carll Ladd and Karlyn H. Bowman, *Attitudes Toward Economic Inequality* (Washington, D.C.: AEI Press, 1998), 36–37.

40. Ibid., 99; Humphrey Taylor, "Harris Poll," Gannett News Service, January 14, 1996.

41. U.S. Department of Commerce, Economics, and Statistics Administration, "Poverty Rates by Age: 1959–1996," a chart in "Income, Poverty, and Health Insurance: 1996," U.S. Bureau of the Census, 1997; Leatha Lamison-White, U.S. Bureau of the Census, Current Population Reports, Series P60-198, *Poverty in the United States: 1996* (Washington, D.C.: U.S. Government Printing Office, 1997), v.

42. Mayer and Jencks, "Has Poverty Really Increased Among Children Since 1970?" tables 2 and 3; David Whitman, "The Poor Aren't Poorer," *U.S. News & World Report*, July 25, 1994, 33–38.

43. Mayer and Jencks, "Has Poverty Really Increased Among Children Since 1970?" table 3.

44. Leif Jensen, David J. Eggebeen, and Daniel T. Lichter, "Child Poverty and the Ameliorative Effects of Public Assistance," *Social Science Quarterly,* vol. 74, no. 3 (September 1993), 557; Whitman, "The Poor Aren't Poorer," 33.

45. Mayer and Jencks, "Has Poverty Really Increased Among Children Since 1970?" 21.

46. Kathleen Short and Martina Shea, Economics and Statistics Administration, "Beyond Poverty, Extended Measures of Well-Being: 1992," Current Population Reports, Household Economic Studies, P70-50RV, U.S. Bureau of the Census, November 1995, 1.

47. Bruce Barlett, "How Poor Are the Poor?" *American Enterprise,* January/February 1996, 58. Data on appliance ownership in the United States in 1971 come from W. Michael Cox and Richard Alm, "By Our Own Bootstraps: Economic Opportunity and the Dynamics of Income Distribution," *1995 Federal Reserve Bank of Dallas Annual Report,* 22.

48. Short and Shea, "Beyond Poverty," 2, 3.

49. Mayer and Jencks, "Has Poverty Really Increased Among Children Since 1970?" table 8. See also Susan Mayer and Christopher Jencks, "War on Poverty: No Apologies, Please," *New York Times,* November 9, 1995.

50. Christopher Jencks, *The Homeless* (Cambridge, Mass.: Harvard University Press, 1994), 16–17.

51. Humphrey Taylor, "Harris Poll," Gannett News Service, January 14, 1996. The January 14, 1996, column by Taylor summarized trends in the Harris poll's "Alienation Index." One question that the index tracks is "Do you tend to feel or not feel that the rich get richer and the poor get poorer?"

52. Cited in Everett Carll Ladd, ed., *America at the Polls: 1994* (Storrs, Conn.: Roper Center for Public Opinion Research, 1995), Occasional Papers and Monographs Series, no. 2, 36.

53. Ruy A. Teixeira and Joel Rogers, "Who Deserted the Democrats in 1994?" *American Prospect,* no. 23 (fall 1995), 75.

CHAPTER SEVEN: Slowing the Alarmism Cycle

1. Julian Simon, ed., *The State of Humanity* (Oxford, England, and Cambridge, Mass.: Blackwell, 1995), 657.

2. Aaron Wildavsky, *Searching for Safety* (New Brunswick, N.J.: Transaction Publishers, 1988), 91.

3. It is worth noting in passing that arrests of juveniles for violent crime—after rising rapidly from 1988 to 1994—declined from 1994 to 1996. For every 100,000 youths ages 10 to 17, 465 were arrested for a violent crime in 1996—still well above the 334 per 100,000 arrested in 1980. Howard N. Snyder, "Juvenile Arrests 1996," Office of Juvenile Justice and Delinquency Prevention, U.S. Department of Justice, November 1997, 1–9. Despite the rise in violent juvenile crime, news stories that warn of a looming wave of "superpredators" often exaggerate the prevalence of violent juveniles. Less than 0.5 percent of all persons age 10 to 17 are arrested for a violent crime in a given year, and more than 90 percent of all juvenile crime does not involve violence.

Statistics on murders by strangers are notoriously unreliable. But murders classified by law enforcement agencies as stranger homicides have declined markedly in the last several years. In 1993, 3,259 stranger homicides were reported to the Federal Bureau of Investigation; in 1996, 2,321 stranger homicides were reported to the FBI, a drop of about 30 percent. See table 2.12 from Federal Bureau of Investigation, *Crime in the United States: 1993* (Washington, D.C.: U.S. Government Printing Office, 1994) and table 2.12 in the 1996 edition.

4. "Why Don't Americans Trust the Government?" *Washington Post*/Kaiser Family Foundation/Harvard University Survey Project, 1996, Henry J. Kaiser Family Foundation, Menlo Park, Calif., 1996, 24.

5. ABC News poll, April 30–May 6, 1996, retrieved from Public Opinion Online, Roper Center for Public Opinion Research, University of Connecticut at Storrs. Twenty-two percent of the adults polled by *ABC News* who rated the crime problem bad or very bad said they based their rating on personal experience.

6. Gregg Easterbrook, *A Moment on the Earth: The Coming Age of Environmental Optimism* (New York: Viking, 1995). Gregg Easterbrook, "The Good Old Days," *Los Angeles Times,* November 5, 1995.

7. Gregg Easterbrook, "Ignore All Doomsayers on EPA Laws," *Los Angeles Times,* December 1, 1996; William Booth, "In L.A., a Clear Day Is a Dream No Longer," *Washington Post,* December 18, 1997.

8. U.S. Environmental Protection Agency, *National Air Quality and Emissions Trends Report, 1995,* Office of Air Quality Planning and Standards, Research Triangle Park, N.C., EPA 454/R-96-005, October 1996, 1–4.

9. "Why Don't Americans Trust the Government?," 4.

10. Center for Media and Public Affairs, "1997 Year in Review: TV's Leading News Topics, Reporters, and Political Jokes," *Media Monitor,* vol. 12, no. 1, (January/February 1998), 1–2. Daniel Amundson, research director for the Center, reports that network evening news aired 104 stories on murder in 1992; by comparison, they aired 486 murder stories in 1997 (after excluding coverage of the O. J. Simpson case).

11. David Whitman, "A Bad Case of the Blues," *U.S. News & World Report,* March 4, 1996, 54.

12. Ibid.

13. David W. Moore, "Americans' Most Important Source of Information: Local TV News," *Gallup Poll Monthly,* September 1995, 2–8; Louis Harris and Associates, "Public's Perceptions of the Media," conducted for Center for Media and Public Affairs, survey questionnaire with marginals, December 1996, 6.

14. Paul Klite et al., "Baaad News: Local TV News in America, 2/26/97," Rocky Mountain Media Watch, Denver, Colo., Content Analysis no. 9, 10. See also "National Survey Finds Crime Dominates Local TV News," University of Miami at Coral Gables, news release of findings by the Consortium for Local Television Surveys, dated May 6, 1997.

15. Stephen Seplow and Jonathan Storm, "The Small Screen Frames the Debate," *Philadelphia Inquirer,* December 1, 1997.

16. "Television's Credibility . . . ," *American Enterprise,* September/October 1997, 92.

17. David Finkel, "At the Lake," *Washington Post Magazine,* June 25, 1995,

13; Shelley Levitt, "Portrait of a Killer," *People,* November 21, 1994, 58; Charles Derber, *The Wilding of America* (New York: St. Martin's Press, 1996), 31–34.

18. Quoted in Derber, *The Wilding of America,* 33.

19. Louis Harris and Associates, "Public's Perceptions of the Media," conducted for Center for Media and Public Affairs, survey questionnaire with marginals, December 1996, 12–13.

20. Albert C. Gunther, "Overrating the X-Rating: The Third-Person Perception and Support for Censorship of Pornography," *Journal of Communication,* vol. 45, no. 1 (winter 1995), 28–39.

21. Linda Heath and John Petraitis, "Television Viewing and Fear of Crime: Where Is the Mean World?" *Basic and Applied Social Psychology,* vol. 8, nos. 1 and 2, (1987), 122.

22. Albert C. Gunther and Paul Mundy, "Biased Optimism and the Third-Person Effect," *Journalism Quarterly,* vol. 70, no. 1 (spring 1993), 58.

23. Fathali M. Moghaddam and Charles Studer, "The Sky Is Falling, but Not on Me: A Cautionary Tale of Illusions of Control, in Four Acts," *Cross-Cultural Research,* vol. 31, no. 2 (May 1997), 155–67; Richard Morin, "The Discrimination Paradox," *Washington Post* ("Unconventional Wisdom" column), December 14, 1997.

24. Glenn Hodges, "When Good Guys Lie," *Washington Monthly,* January/February 1997, 30; David Whitman, "Missing Children: What Makes Search So Tough," *U.S. News & World Report,* August 19, 1985, 60–62.

25. Paul Ehrlich, *The Population Bomb* (New York: Ballantine, 1971 ed.), xi.

26. Paul Ehrlich, "Eco-Catastrophe," *Ramparts,* vol. 24, no. 8 (1969). Ehrlich also said in 1969, "I would take even money that England will not exist in the year 2000." Michael Fumento, *Washington Times,* January 13, 1998.

27. Paul Ehrlich and Anne Ehrlich, "Starvation: 1975," *Penthouse,* July 1975.

28. Paul Ehrlich, *The Population Bomb,* 179. See also John Maddox's critique of Ehrlich in *The Doomsday Syndrome* (New York: McGraw-Hill, 1972), 19.

29. Quoted in Hodges, "When Good Guys Lie," 35. Ehrlich offers a similar justification for alarmism in Michael Wines, "The Sky Is Falling: Three Cheers for Chicken Little," *New York Times,* December 29, 1996.

Advocates like Ehrlich aren't alone in resorting to alarmism. Eban Goodstein and Hart Hodges carefully document that industry lobbyists and government economists have consistently grossly overestimated the costs of proposed environmental regulations for reducing pollution from absestos, benzene, chlorofluorocarbons, coke ovens, cotton dust, halons, strip mining, and vinyl chloride. Eban Goodstein and Hart Hodges, "Polluted Data: Overestimating Environmental Costs," *American Prospect,* November/December 1997, 64–69.

30. By the end of 1997, population experts had started arguing over whether the population explosion had ended. Ben J. Wattenberg, "The Population Explosion Is Over," *New York Times Magazine,* November 23, 1997, 60; and "Population," an online exchange between Wattenberg and Kenneth Hill, in *Slate* (on paper), January 9, 1998, 28–30.

31. David Whitman, "Shattering Myths About the Homeless," *U.S. News & World Report,* March 20, 1989, 27–28.

32. Anastasia Toufexis, "Crack Kids," *Time,* May 13, 1991, 56–63; Jerry Adler, "Hour by Hour: Crack," *Newsweek,* November 28, 1988, 64–79; Barbara Kantrowitz, "The Crack Children," *Newsweek,* February 12, 1990. The pessimism of the early stories on crack babies is much more tempered in later years. See, for example, Sharon Begley, "Hope for 'Snow Babies,' " *Newsweek,* September 29, 1997, 62–63.

33. Hodges, "When Good Guys Lie," 32. For a fuller recounting of crack cocaine's impact on infants and the media treatment of crack, see Susan Fitzgerald, "Coming Up With the 'Wrong' Answer: The 'Crack Baby' Reports were Horrifying. But Were They True?" *Philadelphia Inquirer* (Sunday Magazine), June 15, 1997; and Gary A. Emmett, "What Happened to the 'Crack Babies'?" *Drug Policy Analysis Bulletin,* Federation of American Scientists, No. 4, February 1998, 1–3.

34. Hodges, "When Good Guys Lie," 32.

35. Ibid., 32–33.

36. Contrary to the stereotype, stay-at-home moms at the turn of the century did not spend quiet evenings reading in front of the fire, devote lots of attention to their children, cook savory meals, and enjoy other homespun virtues. In 1900, families took less than two days of vacation a year, and preparing the simplest meal was a time-consuming chore. The average housewife baked over half a ton of bread a year (about 1,400 loaves) and in a typical week spent about 44 hours preparing meals and cleaning them up, another 7 hours or so on laundry, and an additional 7 hours on cleaning—roughly a 60-hour workweek. Americans drank much more than today; on average they consumed about 23 drinks a week, 11 of hard liquor, 12 glasses of beer, plus an occasional glass of wine or chaser. Private, indoor toilets were a luxury; in 1910, 46 percent of whites born in the United States had to share toilets. Stanley Lebergott, *Pursuing Happiness* (Princeton, N.J.: Princeton University Press, 1993), 51, 81, 88, 99.

Because families were much larger in 1900 than today, the typical mother washed a stunning 40,000 diapers on scrub boards while her children were young, compared to a mom today who might wash 1,500 diapers—if she didn't use disposables (Lebergott, *Pursuing Happiness,* 60). Americans' large families also meant that mothers, even as late as the 1920s, spent *less* time caring for each of their children than mothers do today. David Whitman, "The Myth of AWOL Parents," *U.S. News & World Report,* July 1, 1996, 54–56. Otto Bettmann, the founder of the famed Bettmann photo archive in New York, wrote a droll book in the 1970s that assails the idea that the turn of the century was an age of innocence. See Otto L. Bettmann, *The Good Old Days—They Were Terrible!* (New York: Random House, 1974).

37. Ted J. Smith, *The Vanishing Economy: Television Coverage of Economic Affairs, 1982–1987* (Washington, D.C.: Media Institute, 1988), 39.

38. Quoted in Nicholas Lemann, "It's Not as Bad as You Think It Is," *Washington Monthly,* March 1997, 12.

39. Ibid., 13.

40. Jacob Weisberg, *In Defense of Government: The Fall and Rise of Public Trust* (New York: Scribner, 1996), 168.

41. "It's Been a Good Project," interview of Jimmy Carter by staff writer Elizabeth Kurylo, *Atlanta Constitution,* September 15, 1996.

42. Gary M. Pomerantz, "The Atlanta Project: Five Years Later; Great Expectations, Humbling Reality," *Atlanta Constitution,* September 15, 1996.

43. Ibid.

44. Ibid.

45. Richard Berke, "Americans Foresee Harmony in Capital," *New York Times,* January 20, 1997.

46. Ibid.

47. Daniel Katz et al., *Bureaucratic Encounters: A Pilot Study in the Evaluation of Government Services* (Ann Arbor, Mich.: Survey Research Center, Institute for Social Research, University of Michigan, 1975). As Katz pointed out in 1975, it is hard for most people to overcome the stereotype of inefficient bureaucrats and corrupt politicians conveyed by the media. The disjunction between people's "good" personal experience with government agencies and their dim opinion overall of government still holds true. In 1996, only 18 percent of adults said that personal experience was the "most important" influence in forming their impression of the federal government; 72 percent cited television, newspaper, and other media as the most important source of their impressions of the federal government. "Why Don't Americans Trust the Government?" 14.

48. Mickey Kaus, *The End of Equality* (New York: Basic Books, 1992), 77–102.

49. Lawrence Otis Graham, *Proversity* (New York: Wiley, 1997).

50. Kaus, 80–97, 121–35.

51. John Brehm and Wendy Rahn, "Individual-Level Evidence for the Causes and Consequences of Social Capital," *American Journal of Political Science,* vol. 41, no. 2 (April 1997), 1,017; Richard Morin and Dan Balz, "Americans Losing Trust in Each Other and Institutions," *Washington Post,* January 28, 1996.

52. Sherry Turkle, interview with author, January 1997.

53. David Whitman, "Fixing the Welfare Mess," *U.S. News & World Report,* December 13, 1993, 30–34.

Not long ago, Gerald Greenwald, the chief executive officer of United Airlines Corporation, became chairman of the nonprofit "Welfare to Work Partnership," which the Clinton administration helped establish to encourage private businesses to hire hundreds of thousands of welfare recipients. Greenwald found early on that many businesses were not eager to hire from the welfare rolls. As he lamented at a White House ceremony with President Clinton and Vice President Gore, "We can never be a great nation with a philosophy of 'I'm okay, tough luck for you,' " Peter Baker, "Businesses Pledge to Aid Shift from the Dole to Payroll," *Washington Post,* May 21, 1997.

54. From Samuel Johnson's 1812 *Sermons,* quoted in David G. Myers, *Social Psychology,* 2nd ed. (New York: McGraw-Hill, 1987), 102.

1. John Milton, *Paradise Lost*. Quoted in John Marks Templeton, *Is Progress Speeding Up?* (Philadelphia, Pa.: Templeton Foundation Press, 1997), 167.

2. The July 1995 cover of the *Atlantic Monthly* was headlined: "The Crisis of Public Order." Its subhead stated: "We have fled our cities. We have permitted the spread of wastelands ruled by merciless killers. We have abandoned millions of our fellow citizens to every kind of danger and degraded assault. And now a demographic surge is about to make everything worse." Adam Walinsky, "The Crisis of Public Order," *Atlantic Monthly*, July 1995, 39–54.

The political scientist John Mueller has more broadly critiqued the news coverage of the *Atlantic Monthly*. In a 1997 talk, he said, "The *Atlantic* seems addicted to articles like 'the Crisis of Public Order,' 'The Drift Toward Disaster,' 'The Coming Anarchy,' and 'The Coming Plague' . . . the editors will only be truly happy, some suggest, when they will proudly be able to feature an article entitled, 'World Ends, Experts Say.'" John Mueller, "The Rise of the Politically Incorrect One-Handed Economist," January 6, 1997, Department of Political Science at the University of Rochester, paper prepared for the Festschrift in Honor of Richard Rosecrance, Palm Springs, Calif., January 24–26, 1997.

3. Letter from William Whitworth to author, February 14, 1996. Whitworth's typically gracious note did offer that the piece provided "some needed balance in our picture of what's happening in the country."

4. Arthur Herman, *The Idea of Decline in Western History* (New York: Free Press, 1997), 447–48.

5. Stephanie J. Ventura et al., Centers for Disease Control and Prevention, "Births and Deaths: United States, 1996," *Monthly Vital Statistics Report*, National Center for Health Statistics, vol. 46, no. 1, supplement 2, September 11, 1997, 5.

6. A 1993 Roper poll asked adults whether they would like "to change certain things about themselves . . . or do you like it [your life] the way it is?" Most respondents said, "I like it as it is": 90 percent desired to keep their first name or nickname, 88 percent wanted to maintain the friends they regularly saw, 85 percent liked their current family life, 76 percent wouldn't change their social class, and 69 percent liked their overall appearance. "I Like My Life Pretty Well as It Is, Thank You," *Public Perspective*, August/September 1995, 37. Even when people are asked to contemplate switching roles with a famous author or movie star—John Updike, Warren Beatty, Ted Koppel, and so on—most individuals are reluctant to make the switch. Thomas Gilovich, *How We Know What Isn't So* (New York: Free Press, 1991), 75–76.

7. Americans routinely complain about how "negative" the press is. In 1996, 90 percent of the public thought the news media were more likely to report "bad news about terrible, violent crimes," compared to 7 percent who thought the media were more likely to report the "good news that violent crime is decreasing." Humphrey Taylor, "Why Is Public Opinion So Gloomy and Negative? (Part II). It's the Media, Stupid!" The Harris poll 1996, Louis Harris and Associates, New York, release no. 33, May 27, 1996.

Yet when media outlets seek to promote more balanced coverage of the "good news," readers and viewers often are disinterested. See Dana Milbank,

"Here's Good News! And if We're Right, You Won't Read It," *Wall Street Journal,* March 31, 1997; Michael Winerip, "Looking for an 11 O'Clock Fix," *New York Times Magazine,* January 11, 1998, 30–39, 50.

8. The tenor of public opinion in 1997 was well captured in two mid-year polling round-ups. Frank Newport of the Gallup Poll concluded that the public's "mood is no more positive, and in fact is actually less positive than at several other points in time within the last 15 years." Frank Newport, "Americans Upbeat, But Not Extraordinarily So," *Gallup Poll Monthly,* May 1997, 15.

Roper Starch reported that "Americans feel much better today than they did in the early to mid-1990s, when the nation was slogging through a recession and waves of corporate downsizings . . . But these aren't the best of times. . . . while Americans are feeling more optimistic about the future of these things than they did two years ago, they have felt better about them at different times in the past. On a half-dozen occasions in the 1970s and 1980s, 60 percent or more of the public was optimistic about [the] quality of life in the nation, including a high of 65 percent in 1983, 12 points higher than the current reading. Similarly, an average of 50 percent of the public in the 1970s and '80s was optimistic about the public schools, 7 points higher than the current reading and 18 points higher than 1995's nadir of 32 percent. On the system of government, an average of 51 percent of people were optimistic in the '70s and '80s, 11 points higher than the current measure."

Roper Starch concluded: "The current sense of good feelings comes closest to the highs of the past when people are asked to assess how things are going for them personally. Some 79 percent of Americans say the past year has been 'very good' (19 percent) or 'fairly good' (60 percent) for them personally. That figure, 13 points lower than the recession low (reached in 1992), is only 2 points lower than the record (reached twice in the 1970s and once in the '80s)." Roper Starch, "Better—But Not 'The Best of Times,'" *Public Pulse,* vol. 12, no. 8, August 1997, 1, 7.

9. A search of Public Opinion Online at the Roper Center at the University of Connecticut found nine national polls during 1997 where less than half of those surveyed thought the country was moving in the right direction. However, a tenth poll taken in December 1997 showed a majority of Americans (60 percent) thought the country was moving in the right direction. Chuck Raasch, Gannett News Service, "Poll on How America's Doing Finds Rampant Ambiguity," *Idaho Statesman,* December 25, 1997.

When a June 1997 ABC News poll asked people to compare life for the next generation of Americans with life today, more respondents thought it would be worse in the future than thought it would be better. In a February 1997 Yankelovich Partners poll for *Time*/CNN, 67 percent of adults thought that the next generation of children would be worse off economically than the current generation. (Both polls retrieved from Public Opinion Online.)

10. Richard Morin, "The Sunny Side of Scandal," *Washington Post,* February 8, 1998, and Morin and Deane, "Poll Shows More Citizens Satisfied With Government," *Washington Post,* January 21, 1998.

11. See Morin, "The Sunny Side of Scandal."

Other articles reporting poll results from 1998 that show a rise in public optimism about the direction of the country include Dan Balz and Claudia Deane, "Poll Finds Impatience with Starr," *Washington Post,* April 5, 1998; Robert Samuelson, "Why Clinton Hangs On," *Washington Post,* April 1, 1998; Ronald G. Shafer, "Washington Wire," *Wall Street Journal,* March 6, 1998; David Lauter, "U.S. Public Backs Strike on Iraq, Poll Finds," *Los Angeles Times,* February 2, 1998; and Richard Morin, "President's Popularity Hits a High," *Washington Post,* February 1, 1998.

12. Richard L. Berke, "Clinton's O.K. in the Polls, Right?" *New York Times,* February 15, 1998. Berke reviewed a CBS News poll that showed 50 percent of Americans said they themselves were "not at all interested" in the news stories on President Clinton's sex life, 37 percent allowed that they were "mildly curious," and 7 percent confessed that they were "fascinated." When asked, however, to rate *other* people's interest in Clinton's sex life, just 18 percent of the public thought other people had no interest in the news stories, 49 percent said they were mildly curious, and 25 percent said others were fascinated by the stories. This "It's Not Me-It's Them" gap, as the *Times* put it, was particularly wide for women. Only 2 percent of women said they personally were fascinated by the news stories but 23 percent of the women polled thought that other people were fascinated by the stories.

13. Quoted in Greg Pierce, "Inside Politics," *Washington Times,* September 23, 1997. Bennett spoke at a 1997 forum at the conservative Heritage Foundation.

14. Charles Dickens, *American Notes,* originally published in 1842 (New York: Modern Library, introduction by Christopher Hitchens, 1996 ed.), 322.

15. Louis Harris and Associates, May 1–5, 1997 poll of 1,034 adults, retrieved from Public Opinion Online, Roper Center for Public Opinion Research, University of Connecticut at Storrs, load date June 3, 1997. A 1998 poll by Lake Sosin Snell Perry & Associates for the National Partnership for Women and Families shows that the belief that crime is getting worse continued into 1998. Fifty-six percent of the 1,115 adults surveyed thought crime was getting worse; only 27 percent thought it was getting better. Lake Sosin Snell Perry & Associates, "Family Matters: A National Survey of Women and Men," Topline Report, February 1998, 3.

16. "What the Public Understands About Health Stories in the News," Kaiser/Harvard Health News Index, vol. 2, no. 5, September/October 1997, Henry J. Kaiser Family Foundation, Menlo Park, Calif. The AIDS death rate will almost surely continue to plummet in 1997. During the first half of 1997, 12,040 people died from AIDS in the United States, a drop of 44 percent from the first six months of 1996, when 21,460 people died. Thomas H. Maugh II, "U.S. AIDS Deaths Fall 44%; New Cases Drop," *Los Angeles Times,* February 3, 1998.

17. Ronald G. Shafer, "Washington Wire," *Wall Street Journal,* December 12, 1997.

INDEX